From Child Actor to Serial Killer : The True Story of Skylar Julius Deleon

Pete Dove

Published by Trellis Publishing, 2021.

While every precaution has been taken in the preparation of this book, the publisher assumes no responsibility for errors or omissions, or for damages resulting from the use of the information contained herein.

FROM CHILD ACTOR TO SERIAL KILLER : THE TRUE STORY OF SKYLAR JULIUS DELEON

First edition. July 3, 2021.

Copyright © 2021 Pete Dove.

ISBN: 979-8224563272

Written by Pete Dove.

FROM CHILD ACTOR TO SERIAL KILLER

THE TRUE STORY OF JULIUS SKYLAR DELEON

The Child Star Who Shined Dull

Some crimes are so vile that they stick in the mind. Attacks on children, assaults on the elderly. Skylar Deleon's murder of a middle-aged couple fits into this category. It is one of the coldest, most mindlessly cruel killings in the history of the US.

Skylar Deleon considered his victims' lives in the way most of us regard the wrapper off a chocolate bar. It does a job, but when the luscious center it protects has provided its short-term thrill, it is thrown away, disregarded. Not with any purpose, or any intent, but just because it is no longer needed.

Skylar Deleon and his small crew of cronies murdered Jackie and Thomas Hawks by tying them to the anchor of their yacht, then pushing that heavy anchor over the side, dragging them to an inevitable death by drowning. His motive was pure greed. He wanted the yacht, and if Skylar Deleon wanted something he could not get legitimately, he liked to take it anyway. Never mind the cost.

Deleon was born John Julius Jacobson Jr on August 12th, 1979 in Sun Valley, California. This neighborhood of Los Angeles is one of the poorer in both the city and the county, and also one of the least educated. It is ethnically diverse, with a heavy percentage of people of Latino heritage living in its boundaries.

To the south of the neighborhood lies the region of North Hollywood, and it was towards Hollywood that young John Julius turned his small features and neatly parted mousey coiffure. He was a good-looking boy, there is no doubt of that. Small for his age – his tiny stature would later play a part in the murder of the Hawks – with all American looks, he was a natural for the advertising industry.

It is easy to think back and picture these TV advertisements of thirty years ago; upbeat, lots of music and dancing, whatever object being flogged presented in bright, technicolor glory. It was a false world that those late eighties and early nineties advertisements presented. If copies of the sets which featured his toothy, wide smiling face still exist, they do so only in the fading video cassettes of those involved in their production. Skylar Deleon was not, by any means, a star.

If the advertisements liked to create a sugar-coated fantasy world of plenty and enthusiasm, then young Skylar was a perfect actor for them, however. Because his own world was no more than a sugar-coated shell; albeit one with a lot of unhappiness underneath.

It seems as though the boy was a much less willing participant in the development of a burgeoning acting career than his father, John Julius Jacobson senior. Later, when on trial for his life, Deleon's defense team would look to use a childhood filled with abuse as an explanation for their client's apparently psychopathic personality.

Deleon himself talked about being picked up from school to be dragged from one audition to another, frequently beaten by having his hair pulled or his arms thumped by a father who saw his son as a route towards the riches a successful acting career would bring.

Of Deleon's mother, Lisa Wildin, little is said. But his father's abuse was regular and wide ranging. Later, the man would die early, a victim of the AIDS epidemic which first swept the United States in the 1980s and early 1990s. There were further hints from Deleon that the abuse had escalated beyond the physical, with possible sexual attacks added to the charge sheet he would have liked to bring against his violent and predatory father.

Gary Pohlson, the attorney leading for the defense in Deleon's trial, said 'He's had a horrible, horrible life,' in an (ultimately failed) attempt to evoke some sympathy in the jury.

There were plenty, though, as well as the jury, who doubted the defense team's story. It is easy, they said, to make allegations against a dead man, especially of wrongdoing that happened in private, with the only witnesses the victim and the perpetrator. That alleged perpetrator could do nothing to defend himself now.

Others argued that this sense of being the victim was a part of Deleon's personality, a trait which saw him unwilling to accept responsibility for what he had done.

However, that trial lay in the future. Young Skylar continued to attend numerous auditions for commercials, to be rejected mostly but accepted occasionally. He was a good-looking boy, as we have said, but perhaps not quite good looking enough for the sugary sweet advertising market of those days. His slightly protruding front teeth worked for some directors, but not for others. Maybe his father was too pushy at auditions, and Skylar found production teams wary of taking a risk on him, especially when child actors were abundantly available in the area.

There was one more reason for the rejections. Skylar wasn't very good. He was slow to learn moves, found concentration hard to maintain, was immature for his age. Although his small size meant that he could be used to play younger children, an attribute often welcome in the child acting world, his additional years did not offer much in the way of additional quality. Certainly, even back then, there were working restrictions dependent on age, so older kids could work for longer hours than younger ones, but the difference was not enough to often swing a part in his favor.

It was a very crowded market, and Skylar failed to rise about the swathe of good looking mediocrity which had encouraged pushy parents to launch their sunny faced prodigy into a cut throat world where false expectations reigned, and rose colored assessments of their kids' dubious talents cut nothing among hard nosed directors and casting agents.

Then, when he was fourteen (but still looked eleven) Skylar got his break. Not his big break, note (despite what he would later claim) but a move out of the limited world of TV commercials. He won a part in a spin off film from the Power Rangers franchise, a series of GI Joe type toys popular in the 1980s. These had, like many other icons of modern youth culture, been turned into a TV series, and morphed into a film, 'Mighty Morphin Power Rangers: The Movie'. The production was a financial success even if it was a critical tomato (of the rotten variety). It was one of the top grossing films of its release period, and covered most of its $15 million budget in its first weekend, packing movie theatres with screaming pre-teens, and no doubt making cinema chains a fortune from their sale of sugary drinks and oversized cartons of popcorn.

However, as a critical success, the film was what it was – such gaffes as mysterious warriors appearing from nowhere bothering its young target audience not a whit, even if they evoked a smile among otherwise bored critics.

Yet the film's success (or otherwise) owed little to Skylar Deleon. The boy had an uncredited walk on part. A role which maybe earned him $100 or $150, a fee most probably taken by his father at any rate. The outrageous boasts he later made that the sums he earned as a child actor would allow him to purchase a half a million dollar yacht, in cash, with plenty of change in the bank, were certainly not backed up by his role in this film.

No doubt Deleon's father, maybe even the boy himself, hoped that he would now have the doors to a Hollywood future opened for him. His resume would glow under the glittering lights of his part in 'Mighty Morphin Power Rangers: The Movie'. Sadly, that was not to be the case. There was a good reason why Deleon's role was a non-speaking one. He could not learn lines. Maybe that was a sign of a learning difficulty, such as dyslexia, maybe a lack of commitment, but it was a handicap when it came to gaining bigger roles in films and TV series. An insurmountable one.

Deleon's career hit the rocks. The one asset he possessed, his youthful looks and pure-bred all-American boy's face, disappeared when puberty finally hit. Unsurprisingly, directors were not interested in under-sized young men who could not learn their lines, even if they could boast a walk on part in the Power Rangers film.

Deleon would need to find other ways of earning a living. The route he chose was not one to admire.

Thomas Hawks was a probation officer and a keen bodybuilder. When he met his second wife, Jackie, the two knew that they were made for each other. Hawks had children from his first marriage, who were in their teens when Jackie came on the scene. Potentially, that is a difficult situation. Teenage kids can be resentful of their parents' new partners, and relationships can stall. That was not the case with Jackie. Loving from the start, tolerant and interested, the kids took her to their hearts, and she became like a mother to them.

Boats had always been a big part of Tom Hawks' life. His kids had grown up with them; little sail boats and the like. They had progressed from an eight-foot dinghy, through to a Boston whaler twice the length. A pontoon boot at twenty feet was followed by a twenty-one-foot Cabo, and finally a twenty-eight-foot Skipjack. When Tom was just seventeen, he had sailed a little fourteen-foot dory out to Catalina Island, and spent his summers as a sailing instructor.

When Matt and Ryan, his two sons came along, they regularly sailed as a family. Twice a year would see longer trips, perhaps in the Gulf of California or all the way around Catalina island. Every other weekend, the family would pack up and head to the coast for a couple of days of sailing.

Tom had been a firefighter but gave that up when his first marriage ended in 1979. He had moved to Prescott, California so that they could be closer to his family. He built his own home and bought a Saloon on the appropriately named Whiskey Row. Indeed, with his bulging muscles and equally large heart, he became an iconic figure in the community. Later, he worked as a Probation officer, supporting those returning to society after a spell behind bars.

He had met Jackie in 1986, at a canoe event on a lake close to where he lived. Their marriage, two years later, had a Hawaiian theme. It was a picture-perfect relationship, as bright and sunny as the shirts they wore on their wedding day. 'My dad thought more of her than anyone,' said his son, Matt. 'They were a perfect couple, like a ship and a rudder. One doesn't work without the other.

Tom had a reputation for fun loving, in the most positive way. His friend was Hal Slaughter, who said: 'You never knew what he was going to do. Afterwards he'd stare at you with those penetrating eyes, and all of a sudden laugh and slap you on the back.'

There was a fourth aspect to Tom's life, beyond Jackie, his sons and his love of the water. That was his body building. 'He was as religious about that as he was about keeping his boat clean,' said Hal. 'And this is no joke, if you walked on his boat with wet feet Tom would be right behind you with a rag, wiping it up.'

For Tom and Jackie, the call of the ocean was great. So great that they determined to retire early. Tom's philosophy on life was a good, honest one said Matt. 'Be honest, work hard. Buy your toys with cash.'

The toy the couple wanted more than anything else was a boat big enough to sail the oceans. Then, in 2001, a little earlier than they had planned, the ideal boat hit the market. A fifty-five-foot trawler called 'Well Deserved.' Which it was. The boat was filled with teak staterooms. The cockpit was spacious and perfect for the couple. Most of all, with a range of two and half thousand miles, the Well Deserved offered the Hawks' the freedom for which their adventurous spirit yearned. Tom approached his sons, to tell them the news he hoped they would appreciate. 'The sea was calling us, and we can't wait any longer. Life is too short to put things off, and one cannot discover new oceans unless they have the courage to lose sight of the shore.' Sticking to his philosophy of avoiding debt, Tom and Jackie put their house up for sale to fund the purchase of the yacht. The fifty-four-year probation officer then took early retirement. With Jackie, who was ten years his junior, they bought the Well Deserved and moved in, spending a year refurbishing it. They learned to Scuba dive, and Tom ensured that he had the training and certificates to cope with anything the ocean could throw at them.

Then they were ready for their big adventure. For two years, they lived in paradise. The first big trip was from Long Beach Harbor, California, where they were docked, to the tip of the Californian peninsula, down towards Mexico and back up the coastline.

'They'd go away to sea,' reported Hal Slaughter, 'and come back with shells and stories. They lived a life most of us want to live. No worries. Stop where and when you want.'

They kept in touch with Matt and Ryan through their satellite phone, where they would gush about the joys of living their life in the sun and on the waves. 'They're retired,' said Matt. 'When the weather's good, they swim and kayak every day. "We've got these beautiful beaches. The water's clean," they would tell him.

For the two years following the point they got the boat as they wanted it, they bounced around the Pacific. Nirvana. But then Matt and his wife found they were expecting a child. The thought of becoming grandparents was an even greater pull to the Hawks than the ocean. Paradise was about to take another step forward. It was a tough decision to give up their life on the waves, but not too difficult to make. After all, if they sold their yacht and used the cash to buy a home, they could still afford a boat, albeit a much smaller one. They could then have the double pleasure of getting to know their knew grandchild while still sailing when the opportunity arose.

They decided to put the Well Deserved on the market, asking for $440000 for the refurbished boat. Soon, they got a response. A twenty-five-year-old man, who looked eighteen. Skylar Deleon came down to the harbor, full of stories of his past. He had been a child star; he had been a feature in a number of films including the Mighty

Morphin Power Rangers franchise. He trusted, correctly, that Tom and Jackie would have little knowledge of what he was talking about.

He had, he claimed, hundreds of thousands of dollars put away from those days as a child star. If he wasn't quite Macauley Culkin, then he was almost as famous, and almost as rich.

But Tom was wary. There was something about the baby-faced alleged screen star that struck an out of tune chord with him. Even though Deleon arrived with his advisor, who supported his every word, Tom was uncertain. Yes, he wanted to sell the boat, but he feared he was about to be ripped off.

Tom and Jackie's doubts were well placed. What they did not know was that Deleon's stories of stardom were grossly exaggerated. Even more importantly, they were unaware that Deleon had just served time for armed robbery and the man with him, Alonso Machain, was poorly qualified to be an advisor. Machain was a prison guard whom Deleon had befriended in the Seal Beach prison in the southern part of California.

The two had remained friends when Deleon was released, and Machain had been tempted when the former inmate had approached him with a watertight scheme to get rich. Apparently, it was a scheme that Deleon had already used. Find some wealthy people who were selling an expensive asset, like a boat. Make out that they were buyers, then steal the asset and kill the owners. 'He would go and look for these people, kill them and he would keep whatever money was left. He approached me and said: "Would you like to make a few million dollars?"' recounted Machain later in court.

Deleon saw the advertisement for the boat and decided that here was a target he could take. He and Machain went out and bought handcuffs and stun guns so that they could overpower the owners. He made an appointment to view the luxury yacht.

But what he and Machain saw was something for which they had not prepared. Tom Hawks was not some elderly man, softened by years of living in luxury. Instead he was powerfully built, active and street wise. What they did not know was that, at various times Tom had worked as a wrestler, as a bouncer evicting the drunk and disorderly from bars and clubs and was used to dealing with the criminal element from his days as a probation officer.

Deleon was wary. He was unsure that he and Machain could overpower the man. Twice the criminal duo visited the boat, twice they aborted their plans to steal it. Then Skylar Deleon had something rare for him. A good idea. Tom and Jackie had explained that they were selling the boat so that they could set up home near their son, ready to become doting grandparents to their new grandchild.

Deleon was married, and his wife, the twenty-three-year-old Jennifer, was pregnant. They also had a baby son. So, on the next visit he took along his wife, and soon the Hawks relaxed. They felt that they could trust such an obviously loving family. No man, in Tom's eyes, would risk the future of his unborn child by committing some crime. It was a surprisingly trusting move for the worldly-wise man, but the powerful pull of babies can take people away from making their best judgements.

A few days later Deleon arranged for a final look at the yacht. He asked to be taken on a short cruise, and then if all went well, he would sign the papers and buy the boat. To this end, he took along not only Machain but also his accountant.

The portentously named John F Kennedy was in fact an ex con, one who struggled to recall a telephone number let alone work with telephone number amounts of dollars. But he was a big man, and a violent one who had already served time for attempted murder. With the element of surprise, Deleon was sure that Kennedy could handle Tom Hawks, as big and as strong as he was, leaving himself and Machion to deal with Jackie.

They were miles out to sea when Kennedy struck, approaching Hawks from behind in the confines of the cabin, and putting him in a choke hold. As the older man fought, Jackie screamed and Machain attempted to subdue her with the stun gun. The incompetent crook failed with the weapon, but eventually managed to overpower the smaller woman.

Tom and Jackie were handcuffed and tied up. Blindfolds were put on their frightened faces and they were gagged. Realisng the danger that they were in, Tom attempted to fight back. He kicked out with his right leg, catching Deleon in the groin and driving him down onto the deck. 'He knew what was going on and he pushed back,' said Machain later in court. 'I think it was his right leg, I guess, kicked backwards and Deleon was behind him trying to tie him and Deleon kind of flew back on his back. The third guy (John F Kennedy) took a hard swing to his right temple and basically, it was a pretty hard blow, he (Tom) was having a hard time staying up.'

The Hawks were forced to sign a contract handing over the boat and all its assets to Deleon, in return for their lives. They did so, the only hope that they had, although Jackie Hawks, perhaps sensing what was happening, left a clue that they had signed under duress. She signed her name incorrectly, leaving off the final 's'. Months on, when Deleon produced the contract to justify his ownership of the Well Deserved, officers noted that the final letter of 'Hawks' had been added later and using a different hand. It was another nail in the coffin of his defense.

Shortly after signing, Tom – bound, blindfolded and gagged once more – heard a familiar but terrifying sound. He sensed himself being tied to something new, and realized it was the anchor chain. Next to him, Jackie mumbled through the gag 'I don't want to die. I want to see my grandson.' But struggle as they might the anchor was released, and they were pulled overboard and into the depths. Their bodies were never found.

Back on board, Kennedy in particular was unmoved by the murder he had just committed. He grabbed a beer and began to fish from the back of the boat. Within a couple of days, police began investigating.

It was not like Tom and Jackie to go forty-eight hours without making contact, and both Matt and Ryan began to worry. With Jim, Tom's brother and a former police chief, pulling strings, the boat was soon found by local police and seen to be in a mess. All the valuables were gone. They immediately located Deleon and Jennifer, but the paperwork they produced seemed, at that stage, to be in order. Deleon put on the best performance of his life, portraying a mixture of bewilderment and distress at the disappearance of the 'lovely' couple from whom he had purchased his new yacht.

Sergeant Evan Sailor was a Newport Beach detective 'They were cool as cucumbers,' he recalled. 'This guy was possibly the best pathological liar I've ever met.'

Meanwhile, the pressure on Deleon was mounting. A big question facing police was how the penniless man, living in a converted garage in his parents in law's garden, could afford a fifty-five-foot yacht. Finally, Deleon claimed to admit the truth. He was a drug dealer and had paid for the boat in used dollars from a major deal he had just completed.

Ryan Hawks knew straight away that this claim was rubbish. 'My father took more than \$400000 in unmarked, laundered money across the hood of their car in the dark, and then ran off to Mexico?' he asked in total disbelief.

But the truth began to emerge. Receipts were found on board for purchases of bleach, trash bags and seasickness pills (Kennedy claiming to be a poor traveler, which was how he got Tom into the cabin). The purchases were traced back to Jennifer Deleon. Then a notary admitted that she had fraudulently backdated the purchase documents to before the date of the Hawks' disappearance. She had been paid \$2000 for her work.

Four months after the Hawks were killed, Machain broke and confessed what had happened. It saved him from a death sentence. Jennifer also escaped a capital sentence because she had not been on board during the actual killing, although the jury were satisfied enough of her guilt to deliver a first-degree homicide conviction.

Kennedy and Deleon are still behind bars. Their days are numbered there, however, since soon the lengthy appeals and checks will be complete, and they will face lethal injections.

As for the former child (not very bright) star, the killing of Tom and Jackie was not Deleon's only murder. John Jarvi had been a fellow convict in Seal Beach jail in 2003 and the two served on a working party together. On December 26th, 2003, Jarvi cashed two $25000 checks and called Deleon. Within two hours, witnesses reported the penniless Deleon spending $18000 in $100 bills at a boatyard. He then deposited a further $21000 dollars in the joint account he operated with his wife.

The next morning, another call was made to Deleon from Jarvi, and this time the former actor drove down to Mexico with his cousin Michael Lewis. Later that day, Jarvi's body was discovered, his throat slashed, by a Mexican road. Less than a year later the Hawks would become his second and third murder victims. Deleon was found guilty of the homicide of Jarvi a year into his sentence for the murder of Tom and Jackie.

Maybe the future was not as bright as it looked for the would-be child star back in the late 1980s and early 1990s. For all that, the young boy with the cute looks could not have expected to be facing the death penalty, with three homicides under his belt, by the time he was in his mid-twenties.

The child actor might or might not have craved fame back then. He found it in the end, though. Just not in the manner he expected.

KILLER STRIPPER : THE TRUE STORY OF MECHELE HUGHES

14

JAMES MORRIS

Kent Leppink's death

Kent Leppink was a commercial fisherman from a relatively comfortable background. He had lived several places in Alaska by the time he settled down in Anchorage, and shared a house with Mechele Hughes and another man named John Carlin III.

His body was left on a hiking trail near Hope, Alaska, an hour from Anchorage. He was discovered by utility workers making their way to a job. But perhaps because of the conditions on that remote hillside, or because of the carefulness of the murderers, no physical evidence was found that could have tied anybody to the crime.

What little evidence there was, and common sense, pointed towards Mechele and Carlin, but not enough to bring them to trial. Leppink's death, however, was almost overshadowed by Mechele Hughes' story: a stripper who had perhaps had her boyfriend murdered in cold blood, by her lover. The salacious story gripped headlines around the country when the case went to trial, a full decade after the crime.

The murder

Details of what happened on the day of Kent Leppink's death are difficult to come by, and were only pieced together during the trial-which came after more than a decade of waiting.

What Kent Leppink may or may not have known, was that Mechele had been seeing at least two other men while living with him, including their housemate Carlin. There was also another man named Scott Hilke, who lived in California. According to allegations that later came out at trial, she had been engaged to them all at some point or another, and maintained relationships with all three at the same time.

On May 2nd 1996, Leppink was found dead courtesy of three gunshot wounds from a .44 calibre handgun. He had been shot at point blank range, and according to the pathologists' report had been murdered anywhere between 6 and 48 hours before his body was recovered.

Whether Mechele and Carlin kept their affair a secret is impossible to say, but perhaps it was the threat of it being revealed that led to Leppink's murder. This, at least, was what State Troopers investigating the case believed. They interviewed Hughes, Carlin and Hilke to try to get to the bottom of what had happened but couldn't definitively pin the crime on any one of them, nor on anybody else.

No charges were brought against Hughes, or against anybody else connected to the crime. And because of the lack of any new evidence coming to light, the case went cold.

A breakthrough after a decade

Michele finally faced court only ten years later, in October 2006. While no fresh physical evidence had been unearthed, the State of Alaska's cold case team- just three people, as it happens- had made a breakthrough during an interview with Carlin's son. He had been underage in 1996, and hadn't been allowed to speak to police. His testimony was so damning that charges were brought against both his father and Mechele Hughes.

The cold case team were also able to confiscate Kent's old computer, which gave them important clues going forward in the case. According to Betsy Leppink's interview with NBC in 2008, she described how information on the computer had been vital: "It held information that was very important to both trials," and she added that the technology to access the information simply hadn't been available all those years ago.

The team had recovered emails from the computer which heavily implied that Carlin and Hughes had lured Leppink out to Hope, Alaska that day. The pair had said that they were renting a cabin in the area, and invited Leppink along; but in reality, there was no cabin, no holiday, and no return home for Leppink.

Another startling piece of evidence was a stolen bronze statue, which John Carlin had kept through all the intervening years. "That was very, very big in the trial," Betsy said during her interview. At that point, it had been returned to Betsy and Ken, and sat in their living room. "She [Hughes] stole it from him. They found it just before Carlin's trial on his fireplace mantle in New Jersey." "On the back side of it, our son's name is printed on it," Ken added.

Based on both new and old evidence, as well as testimony from interviews, the cold case team concluded that Hughes had not murdered Leppink; she had persuaded Carlin to shoot him instead. This made her an accomplice, just as guilty and just as liable for his death. He was sent to a prison in Seward, Alaska.

The first trial, however, was of Carlin alone. Between March and April 2007 he was tried, found guilty and sentenced to life in prison. Carlin's conviction convinced prosecutors to go ahead with Hughes' case, because of her involvement in persuading Carlin to act.

A trial after twelve years

Her supposed motive had been money, as motives often are. Leppink's life insurance would have made Michele and Carlin millionaires, and prosecutors argued that this was all the temptation needed for them to kill him. The beneficiary of this insurance was changed only a few days prior to Leppink's death, however, so Hughes wouldn't have received any pay-out at all. Hughes argued that she had, in fact, tried to cancel the policy- not get the money for herself.

One important piece of evidence was a letter, written by Leppink shortly before his murder. In it he told his parents that if he were to die under 'suspicious circumstances', that it was probably Hughes and Carlin who were responsible. In the letter, he told his parents about Hughes' 'split personality' and that while 'the part [he] fell in love with is very beautiful' that his parents had 'to take Mechele down' and 'make sure she is prosecuted.'

The judge- Anchorage Superior Court Judge Philip Volland- allowed the evidence on the basis that it showed the jury how easy Leppink had been to manipulate, which was one of the central points of the case. Prosecutors had argued that Hughes used Leppink in an effort to gain his life insurance, and for this to have made sense, it was necessary to prove Leppink's naivety and easiness to manipulate.

Prosecutor Pat Gullufsen also brought Hughes' character into disrepute during the trial. He claimed that she had been trying her best to imitate the lead character from the movie 'The Last Seduction', where a woman kills her partner and pins the crime on her lover. And while the inclusion of this line of evidence was strange, and pushing the boundaries of what was allowed in court, the judge allowed the jury to consider it. Prosecutors also argued that Hughes had helped Carlin to wash the murder weapon after Leppink's shooting, cementing her guilt.

Her defence attorneys argued that the evidence brought to trial amounted to a witch hunt, and too much emphasis was placed on Hughes' character as opposed to her actions; before sentencing, Hughes had been subjected to two days of questioning and discussion of her past.

A nationally renowned psychologist, however, testified that Hughes showed none of the signs of personality disorders that can lead to aggression, nor did she show any signs of having overcome (or struggled to overcome) guilt from having murdered Leppink. This suggested that Hughes was completely innocent of having either murdered her fiancé, or planned his murder.

Throughout the trial, Hughes' husband had attended in support. During the judge's verdict, Dr. Linehan was sat behind Mechele, shaking his head at the judge's words.

Hughes was found guilty of Leppink's murder just over a year after the trial began, on October 22nd 2007. Early the next year, she was sentenced to a total of 99 years in prison. She was sent to Hiland Mountain Correctional Center, in Eagle River, Alaska.

Speaking with his wife after the trial, Dr. Linehan said that they would "appeal vigorously the decisions by Judge Volland during the trial." He continued, "...there's the Mechele that everyone who knows her and has been around her for years knows. And the Mechele that the prosecution invented, their narrative."

Judge Volland did at least concede that Hughes should be incarcerated close to her family in Washington, but that was scant comfort for the family who believed that the verdict was an extreme miscarriage of justice.

Who had Hughes become since 1996?

Mechele had become a completely different person since the case was first opened. Between Leppink's murder and Hughes' eventual trial, Mechele Hughes had become Mechele Linehan. She had married Dr. Colin Linehan after the events of the case, and settled down to a normal family life, and even earned a Master's degree. The couple had even had a daughter together, who was 8 years old at the time of the trial.

On March 8th, 2008 CBS's *48 Hours* aired a special on her case, with an exclusive interview. She told an entirely different story to the one which had been used against her. Speaking with reporter Susan Spencer, she said "I just feel like there is nothing I can do to make people believe me or make people like me... A witch I may be, but a psychopath I am definitely not."

"Anybody else that knew me or worked with me didn't feel that way," she says. "You tell me how a 22-year-old girl can make grown men do these things." She also spoke about against the attacks on her character: "The only person I agreed to marry was Scott [Hilke]," she said, and she had only agreed to pretend to be engaged for Leppink's parents.

"I think [Leppink] was gay...he could never tell his family he was gay....He was frantic," she told Spencer as a way of making sense of this situation. Her current husband, Dr. Colin Linehan, also spoke with CBS in that same interview. "This whole thing is surreal. [A] nerve-shattering, anxiety-provoking nightmare...the bottom line is that's not who she is." But Linehan still felt sorry for Leppink's parents over the loss of their son. "Their son is dead. You can't take back the dead. I have nothing but sympathy for them."

The other side of the story

The case had always remained fresh in the public imagination, as stories of women who kill often do. The question of Hughes' innocence or guilt made great TV. Her notorious case was featured on numerous TV cable shows, and the way it was portrayed was a world away from the seemingly genuine interviews the Linehan family gave on CBS.

Shortly after Hughes' conviction- on July 27th, 2008- it was featured in an episode of Dateline NBC, and the next year an updated version with new information was aired too. Soon after, Oxygen Network show Snapped showed a special on Hughes' case, as did Investigation Discovery on the ID Channel. The show was titled 'Love and Death in Alaska'. Hughes's case also featured on E! Network's Fatal Beauty: 15 Most Notorious Women, again in 2009.

But aside from profiles of the beautiful woman turned 'murderer', the parents of Kent Leppink told their story on national TV too. In 2008, the couple- along with their two sons, Craig and Ransomappeared on that same episode of Dateline NBC to give their version of the events of that night, twelve years ago.

It wasn't easy. "We are not naive people anymore," Betsy said. "We've been through too much and have seen too much. Today we still cry. It was horrendous hell." And they didn't mince their words nor hide their suspicions when they discussed Hughes: "She was engaged to four guys at one time," Ken told NBC.

Leppink's parents had always maintained that there was something strange about their son's life insurance policy, which had been bought for him (supposedly) by Hughes' family. "The day he called me that his bronze had been stolen, he said, 'Mom, Mechele's grandpa gave us our wedding gift. It's a million dollar insurance policy on my life,'" Betsy said in her NBC interview. "I said, 'Kent, that's insane. No grandpa buys the future husband of his granddaughter a million dollar life insurance policy.' We were scared to death. I said, 'Get out of there — you're in trouble.'"

They had only met Mechele once, but hadn't taken to her. Whatever it was- they couldn't quite put their finger on it- something wasn't right. "I didn't think that she loved him. She showed no sign of affection toward him," Betsy said. "And the drool was running right out of him. She was a beautiful young girl. By the time we were afraid for his life, it was just too late."

"He just didn't want to give up. He said, 'Mom, I want to give it one more chance.'"

They also discussed the letter that they had received from Kent- more of a package, really- and revealed more about it than had come out at trial. Their son had written that it was his "insurance policy", and he wrote that "If I didn't think that things could get a little 'rough' up here, I wouldn't have sent you this. It's not funny to talk about getting killed, but in today's world you have to expect anything."

Kent also told them to take care of his final affairs, and not dwell for too long on his death. But most importantly, he had asked of them to "take Mechele DOWN. Make sure she is prosecuted."

Prison time

Hughes' spent her time in prison wisely. She did her best to acclimatize herself to what was a completely different environment than the one she had been used to. Her first prison job was for 85c. an hour, sewing prison uniforms.

But she couldn't escape completely from prison life. She had to learn how to work the black market, like every other prisoner- but for her, she didn't want drugs or makeup. She mostly used the system to get fresh fruit and vegetables.

A couple of times she got in trouble- and ended up in solitary confinement- because of the goods she used for bartering, like chewing tobacco. But the rest of her time she spent in her own cell, as she wasn't required to share with anyone else.

Later on, to avoid the black market altogether, she got the privilege of being able to order food from Costco and used an iron to make herself paninis. It was small reminders of life on the outside like this that kept her sane, she said in later interviews. She would also pass her time reading magazines like the New Yorker, and whatever books her family and friends would send to her.

After a year in prison, she switched jobs. She became a prison janitor, working the night shift, so as to avoid the drama and conflict that came from working with others. She would work from 10:30pm to 6:30am each night.

Throughout her time in prison, she received letters: thousands of them, all from strangers. Speaking about them to the press, she described how only three of them had been negative; and she wrote back to as many as she could, even the 'hate mail'. She kept some of the letters and cards that she received, and decorated her cell with them.

The most difficult aspect of her imprisonment was being away from her daughter. She had been 8 years old when Hughes went to jail. "I had a woman tell me when I first got there that you could be a mom from jail," she later said; but she found it difficult nonetheless. It was her daughter that inspired her to keep going, and do everything she could to win her freedom.

Hughes' appeal

Hughes never gave up on her freedom, and she was right not to. Her conviction was fully overturned on February 5th, 2010, by the Alaska Court of Appeals. The reversal was based on the improper evidence that had been allowed to influence the jury's decision: testimony on the movie The Last Seduction, and the letter written by Leppink which was read out in court.

"The State's case against Linehan was circumstantial, and the evidence was subject to different interpretations and was hardly overwhelming," Appeals Chief Judge Robert Coats wrote. "We accordingly conclude that Linehan's conviction must be reversed."

"The State's ability to secure a guilty verdict hinged on convincing the jury to view a large number of ambiguous facts in the light most favorable to Linehan's guilt. In this situation, the evidence of Leppink's posthumous accusations may well have been the weight that tipped the jury's decision," Judge David Mannheimmer wrote.

The judgment was passed 3-0. "Many law-abiding people are drawn to characters in literature or in the cinema who are villainous or roguish—even though they would not dream of engaging in the same crimes or misdeeds," wrote Mannheimer on the topic of the inclusion of 'The Last Seduction' as a major point of the prosecution. Mannheimer also wrote in his statement that Leppink's letter alone would have been enough to overturn Hughes' sentence.

This was based on the fact that a murder victim's testimony doesn't allow for questioning of either the maker of that testimony, nor does it allow the accused to defend themselves against what is written. It's also emotional testimony, which can influence the jury negatively and take their mind away from the actual testimony, and the actual evidence, presented at trial.

'It is almost inevitable that the jurors would view Leppink's assertions as at least circumstantial proof of the matters asserted. In other words, the jurors would suspect that Leppink probably knew what he was talking about," according to the appeals court statement made after the decision was overturned. They also wrote that such evidence is particularly damaging in a case based almost solely on circumstantial evidence, as this one had been.

Hughes' three appeal lawyers, Jeff Feldman, Susan Orlansky and former Alaska Supreme Court Justice Alex Bryne, also brought up the fact that her job as a stripper should never have been brought up, for similar reasons, since it could have clouded the jury's judgment and made the case about her character and not the murder. However, the appeal judges dismissed this particular claim.

Carlin's story took another turn as well, when his sentence was overturned too, on January 21st 2015. But this reverse came far too late for him. He had been found found beaten to death by the other inmates at Spring Creek Correctional Center just a year after his initial incarceration. Nobody has ever been charged with his murder, and had maintained his innocence and his appeals until he died.

Release

The district attorney had two choices now that Hughes' sentence had been overturned: she could either be taken to the Alaska Supreme Court and retried, or set free. But on May 11th, 2010, it was decided that she could be released on $250,000 bail. This sum was far beyond the means of Hughes and her family, who couldn't even afford a bail bondsman at $25,000, or ten percent of the total.

Fortunately for Hughes, a Pennsylvanian businessman donated the necessary money. At the same time, local Anchorage strip club owner

Terry Stahlman had offered his premises as collateral against the sum, although this was rejected by Judge Volland.

The businessman, Brian Watt, is a CFO from Chester Springs, Pa. He donated the bail money because of his firm belief in Hughes' innocence, and expected absolutely nothing in return. He was quoted by the Alaska Dispatch News as saying that he wanted to see 'the process play itself out', and Hughes given another trial, but this time, a fair one.

His intention was far from a desire to be in the limelight, and in short newspaper interviews he expressed his desire to not give out details of his own life. "In the simplest sense, I'm an analyst. I build predictive models of consumer behavior for a living. I analyze complex situations for a living, and ... my conclusion (is) she is innocent. One hundred percent," he wrote in an email to the ADN.

"It was as if the Internet hyenas had gathered at the watering hole, and they were going to rip the flesh from her bones, no matter what she said or did," Watt said. At no point had he ever met Hughes, Leppink or Carlin- nor had he ever even been to Alaska. But his conviction and empathy were so firm that he decided to donate the money.

"The narrative that was being told, in the media, on blogs, and reader commentary on the Internet, took on a life of its own," he wrote in the email. "It appeared to me to be impossible for Mrs. Linehan to escape that pre-assembled story." In all fairness to Watt, the case had been overturned for just those reasons. But his donation was nevertheless remarkable.

Perhaps even more surprisingly, Watt wrote in the same email that it hadn't been the first time he had donated bail money to what he deemed to be worthy causes, although he refused to elaborate further. "I guess I could have saved all the money I spent over the years on these type of projects, and retired early but I never wanted to retire anyways, so it's all good," he told the ADN.

It had only been a short two and a half years since she had been sent to prison to begin with. The conditions of her bail were that she had to stay in the local area, and for all intents and purposes remain under house arrest until the date of her trial, which had been set for September that year.

Life goes on

On August 6th 2012, prosecutors finally decided that they would not send Hughes back to court to face trial again.

In speaking to the Alaska Dispatch News since her release, Hughes has expressed her regret at her youth, saying that she was reckless and manipulative in her early 20s, but that she had since changed, and that it had never made her a killer. She has given extensive interviews to newspapers since her release, describing her experience.

She did set some ground rules, however, for her interviews. In her interview with the Fairbanks Daily News-Miner, for instance, she said that the location of her new apartment couldn't be disclosed; but also she stipulated that she didn't want to talk about the case, on the advice of her new defense lawyers. She requested as well that the name of her daughter was not to be published.

Speaking with the Daily News, she spoke of how she felt after she was let go. She was met by her husband and daughter, and a court appointed custodian who helped her reintegrate into normal life. She had agreed with her family that she would stay in a small studio apartment to begin with, and it was in setting this apartment up that she spent most of her time in that first week.

"I had forgotten how soft a bed could be," she told the paper. In those first few days, she indulged in some of her favourite comfort food, a privilege she hadn't had in prison- avocado, mango and sushi. She spent the first week meeting with her family, her new team of lawyers, and just trying to be normal again.

On the topic of her public image, she told the Daily News "[m]y attorneys always told me to be stoic in court, even during the trial: 'Just be stoic.' So I'd sit there and try to be stoic. Which I laugh at now because that got twisted (into) 'Cold, manipulative bitch. Look at her.' No, I was being stoic, that was my stoic look. You got to either laugh or cry at the situation and crying does you no good."

The twisting of her public image had an effect on her that she was eager to speak out about. "You don't know what it's like to be told that you are the devil woman," she said. Her friends and family told her not to let her portrayal in the media affect her. "From the beginning people told me I'm too thin-skinned. 'You need to toughen up. Let it roll off your back like water, you're a duck,'" she said. "I thought I wanted to be like that, for it to not bother me. But it always did."

At the time of writing, Mechele Hughes operates a Laser Clinic in Tacoma, Washington.

SERIAL KILLING STRIPPER: THE TRUE STORY OF ROBYN LINDHOLM

CHELSEA CALBERT

Australia's Most Dangerous Woman

Robyn Lindholm was destined for fame. By the age of 14, this talented, beautiful young woman was already an up-and-comer in the world of Australian figure skating – competing in national ice-skating championships and even performing alongside Olympic legends Torvill and Dean, handpicked by the duo to participate in their sold-out Face The Music world tour.

However, it wasn't her talent on the ice that ensured Lindholm's name would appear on the front page of newspapers for years. Instead, this gorgeous femme fatale will be remembered as a murderer – and potentially, even a serial killer.

The Victorian Supreme Court finally sentenced 43-year-old Lindholm to 25 years in prison for the premeditated murder of her ex-boyfriend, Wayne Amey, in December of 2015 – but then, police began investigating the possibility that Lindholm was behind at least one other death, as well as the possible murder of another past lover.

"She had an uncanny ability to manipulate men," said Chief Crown Prosecutor Gavin Silbert QC, during one of Lindholm's trials.

Always daddy's girl

Born into a wealthy Melbourne family, Lindholm learned at an early age that her good looks and charm could get her anything she wanted. Even her father was powerless to resist. At the age of 11, Lindholm convinced him that she needed a pony. A few years later, a 14-year-old Lindholm demanded pricey skating lessons – and her dad never failed to indulge his daughter's every wish.

While Lindholm relied heavily on her appearance to get ahead, she grew up a fairly hardworking young girl. After excelling at Kilvington Grammar and even at an elite secondary college, Lindholm planned to attend Monash University to study a Bachelor of Science degree. Her love of horses had endured since childhood, and her passion for endurance riding led Lindholm to pursue a career working with animals.

Her bright future began to derail when she accepted a part-time job working in one of the high-roller rooms at the Crown Casino, the Mahogany Room. Even though Lindholm was just a hostess, her long legs and beautiful blonde hair caught the eye of "the Black Prince of Lygon Street." Alphonse Gangitano was an attractive and wealthy underworld crime leader, and Lindholm was unable to resist the allure of the handsome and powerful man's lifestyle of money, sex, and drugs.

Lindholm's demanding nature suited Gangitano just fine. Once again, she was treated like a princess – Gangitano was more than willing to indulge Lindholm's every whim and buy her whatever she desired. When Gangitano was eventually executed in his own home,

Lindholm would need to find another way to maintain the intoxicating lifestyle she'd gotten accustomed to – by whatever means necessary.

Simply Irresistible

While working in the Mahogany Room, Lindholm had developed a relationship with Alex Prelac – a regular customer of the exclusive high-roller room who owned the Simply Irresistible Stripping Agency. Lindholm had purchased her first small farm in Glenhope when she was only 23, and agreed to work part-time for Prelac's agency to help pay down her mortgage.

Stripping not only provided Lindholm with a steady income and the exciting lifestyle she was looking for – it also indulged her need to be the centre of attention. Her job with Simply Irresistible wasn't enough, though. Soon, Lindholm made the jump from stripping to working back in Melbourne's underworld as a highly-paid escort, going by the name "Collette."

John Elder, who worked as editor-in-chief of a magazine that routinely hired strippers for pranks and other comical roles, recalled meeting Lindholm when she was only 20 years old – "an ice-skating champion, newly dropped out of a science degree, moving into animal husbandry."

"She talked to me about her dream of owning her own place in the country, horses, a quiet life," he said. "There was nothing to suggest she'd end up burying one, maybe two boyfriends at the wished-for homestead."

Elder added that for Lindholm, stripping was a "means to a real-estate end," and that as soon as she was able to save enough money, she'd move on to her real passion of working with horses.

Soon after she started at the club, Lindholm struck up a close friendship with another stripper, Shari Davison. Davison was an exotic dancer who had previously worked as a circus trapeze artist, and who had just had a baby when she disappeared after leaving the Crown Casino on a Saturday morning in February of 1995. Her body has never been recovered, but investigations soon began to point to her good friend, Lindholm.

"There were so many rumours, ratbags, and depraved offshoots in our digging around," Elder said. "An inquest in 2001 found that Davison had a taste for drugs, booze, and bad men – and was pronounced mysteriously dead."

Apparently, in the weeks leading up to her disappearance, Davison had confessed to some close friends that she was "in serious trouble" with a gang of young Greeks – a gang which included standover man George Teazis, who had recently started seeing a stripper known as "Collette."

Teazis, also known as Templeton, had once been a member of a Richmond-based gang. The gang participated in the trading of weapons and amphetamines, dubbed the "plastic gangsters." Teazis fell head over heels in love with Lindhom, and even went as far to propose to her and move her into his home. However, he vanished in 2005, shortly after the engagement, and his body remains unfound.

A volatile situation

Two weeks prior to his disappearance, Teazis's brother received an upsetting phone call. Teazis was in tears, distraught over having just caught Lindholm in bed with, presumably, Wayne Amey. According to the brother, the couple had a "violent fight," and Teazis decided to leave Lindholm.

On the day Teazis disappeared, Lindholm had been out with a friend. When she came home, she claims the door was open and Teazis was gone. According to Lindholm, Teazis had sent a text at around 2:30am, stating that he was in some kind of trouble and would need a ride home, but she didn't know where he was.

Tearfully, Lindholm took to the press to express her pain and desire to locate her beloved fiancé. In the meantime, though, she moved all the furniture out of Teazis' home and claimed all of his assets – leaving a small box of toys for her fiancé's grief-stricken teenage son, Ross.

"Ross noticed that his father's F100 campervan was missing, along with his motorbike, a boat, a rear-projection television, jewellery, and other assorted goods worth an uncounted tens of thousands of dollars," said Elder. "Ross says he was so stunned at the time, he immediately went to a friend's home to settle himself. Later, he tried calling (Lindholm), to claim his father's belongings."

According to Ross, Lindholm eventually texted to tell him that she'd left some "clothes and his remote-controlled cars" in boxes on the doorstep. When Ross inquired about the vehicles, Lindholm replied that he would be "getting nothing ... and she forwarded her solicitor's details."

And while Lindholm made a show of crying for the press, Teazis' family members claimed that before getting in front of the cameras, Lindholm had been "laughing with her friend." After shedding some tears during the press conference and mourning the disappearance of her lover, she was "seen laughing again when it was over."

She also chose not to mention her new lover to the TV and newspaper reporters. Before Teazis' disappearance, Lindholm had started an affair with a gym owner named Wayne Amey. With Teazis out of the picture and her stripping career taking off, Lindholm was on track to get everything she ever wanted.

Lindholm reluctanty sold her Glenhope farm to purchase land with Amey, a 10-acre property near Bittern. This would give her plenty of space to pursue her lasting love of equestrianism and, eventually, begin breeding horses. Up until her arrest, Lindholm continued to enjoy endurance riding, and at the time Amey was killed, their property was home to eight beautiful – and expensive – Arabian horses.

Lady Macbeth in Lycra

Although Teazis' body was never recovered, Lindholm was formally charged with his murder in June of 2016. In 2005, police had conceded that it was possible that Teazis may not have wanted to ever be found – but since he hadn't used his mobile phone or accessed his bank accounts, they had "grave concerns."

According to police, Lindholm had convinced her new lover, Amey, to help her kill and dispose of her fiancé – a story that was somewhat corroborated by a strip club owner who had hired Amey as a personal trainer.

"He said (Teazis) was knocking Robyn around," she told Elder. "He kept saying he was going to kill (Teazis). It went on and on. It got scary and I stopped training with him."

The charge came just a few months after Lindholm was convicted of persuading another lover, Torsten "Toots" Trabert, to murder Amey. According to Elder, Lindholm and Amey were separating – and Amey had hoped for a settlement that would leave him half of the couple's rural property.

"Lindholm was angry, vengeful, and bitter over the break-up of her relationship with Amey and the loss of the farm, and he became anxious for his own safety," said a newspaper article published in The Sunday Age, discussing the case.

According to defence barrister John Kelly, Lindholm had "lost everything." Unemployed and living out of her car, she decided her only option was to kill Amey – a man she'd once hoped to start a family with.

"Her sense of grievance at the situation she found herself in needs to be viewed through that prism," Kelly told the Supreme Court following Lindholm's plea of guilt. "She had lost all sense of proportion at that stage. But she blamed Amey for the straights she was in because ... she says she had the most wonderful upbringing and childhood she could hope to have."

Kelly added that by 2013, Lindholm was a "40-year-old woman with no prospect that she could see, no means of support, and no property or assets to her name," but added that none of this information "ameliorates what then happened to Amey."

Despite her desire to see Amey killed, Lindholm knew wouldn't be able to commit the murder on her own. If she wanted her ex-lover dead, she'd need to convince her new lover to do the dirty work. While Lindholm considered her relationship with Trabert to be nothing more than a "fling," he had fallen "madly in love."

"Trabert was infatuated with her," said Chief Crown Prosecutor Gavin Silbert QC, noting that the pair were involved in an "intense sexual relationship." He added that Trabert had even left his wife and children to move in with Lindholm – but there was a price to be paid.

"He couldn't keep his hands off her, and the return for her affection was that he kill Wayne Amey," Silbert said. "It was only with the seduction of Travert that she achieved her aims."

According to Silbert, Trabert wasn't Lindholm's first choice. In fact, he told the Victorian Supreme Court during Lindholm's trial that the stripper had attempted to convince several other former lovers to help her get rid of Amey, but Trabert was the first one to agree to her plan.

However, Trabert did need a bit of persuading. Silbert told the court that Lindholm used her sexuality to seduce Trabert into doing her bidding – to the point where, Silbert said, Trabert was completely obsessed with her. Even while locked in a remand cell following his arrest, Trabert sent flowery love notes to "darling" Lindholm.

"I'm missing you so much that I can't sleep because you are not with me ... we are so good together," one note read. "I can't think of my life without. All my love, Toots."

Trabert ended his note with a carefully drawn heart containing the words "I love you forever."

According to plan

The murder was carried out on December 10, 2013 – the day before Amey and Lindholm were due in court to resolve their dispute over a $1.1 million rural property they owned in Bittern. Lindholm

directed Trabert and his accomplice, John Anthony Ryan, to attack
Amey at his apartment.

The two men beat him repeatedly with a baseball bat, stabbed him,
and choked him – and then wrapped him up and stuffed him in the
trunk of the car. The group then drove to a remote farm in Mt Korong
in Central Victoria, to get rid of Amey's body.

According to court reports, Trabert had tried to find a fourth
person to help the trio "finish off" Amey, but this person refused to get
involved. At this point, records state, Amey could be heard "begging
for his life" from the trunk of the car. When the car was parked at the
farm, Trabert and Ryan completed the murder.

"Post-mortem examination revealed that Amey had multiple stab
injuries to his chest, fractured ribs, pallor and furrow to the left side
of his neck in association with a rope, and multiple lacerations to his
scalp," the court records revealed. "The opinion of the forensic
pathologist was that Amey's death was a result of one or more of these
injuries."

Lindholm kept a watchful eye on her suitor as he and Ryan pushed
the body into a crevice between two rocks, ordering them to use more
rocks and sticks to cover Amey's corpse and ensure it wouldn't be
discovered.

Once the body was sufficiently hidden, Lindholm and Trabert had
sex in the bushes, while Ryan went to a nearby Inglewood hotel to meet
them for drinks. The trio attempted to use Amey's bank cards to clean
out his accounts, and eventually set his vehicle on fire to destroy any
remaining evidence.

"(Lindholm) was laughing and carrying on like it was nothing,"
Ryan told police. "She's on top of the world. They just wanted to
f—-ing party, and I just felt ill, ill the whole way."

Charges laid

Lindholm, Trabert, and Ryan were all apprehended by police just
days after Amey's murder. A car pursuit between Trabert, Lindholm,

and police ended on foot – Trabert was nabbed by police, while Lindholm attempted evade them by crossing a creek. Ryan, meanwhile, was apprehended at a residential address in Coburg after the body was discovered.

"We have found Amey on the top of a hill," said Sen-Constable Philip Gynther, leading homicide detective on the case. "His remains have been place at the bottom of a crevasse between two large rocks. It's been a very long process ... the terrain all looks very similar."

According to court documents, Lindholm pleaded guilty to Amey's murder, while Trabert and Ryan plead their innocence – "each maintaining that it was the other who had killed Amey."

All three received sentences from Supreme Court Justice Lex Lasry – 25 years for Lindholm, 28 years for Trabert, and 31 years for Ryan. According to Lasry, Lindholm had shown "no remorse" for her role in Amey's murder – saying she "no doubt" felt ashamed and embarrassed, but he didn't believe she had a genuine regret for her "bizarre actions" in the "appalling crime."

Lasry also stated the trio had a history of "excessive use" of crystal meth – a drug which tends to fuel "extraordinarily violent criminal behaviour," he said.

While appeals were submitted for reduced terms, Senior Crown prosecutor Douglas Trapnell, QC, said each member of the trio was "equally responsible" for their roles in Amey's murder – whether as an instigator or as a physical killer.

"Because this was a pre-meditated plan and callous killing on the eve of a court hearing, where Amey was to exercise his legal rights, brings it very close to the worst case," Trapnell said. "This man was beaten in the basement of his apartment building where he had the right to feel safe. He was hog-tied ... then put in (a car) boot and remained alive for quite some time, albeit with (injuries including) fractured ribs."

Trapnell also argued that the trio had "desecrated" Amey's body by stuffing it into the crevice on Mt Korong, where, without the assistance of Trabert, it might never have been located. Following his apprehension, Trabert had led police to the farm where Amey's body had been hidden.

"The location of the body by my client allowed the family to seek some closure in having the body returned and afforded a proper burial," said Trabert's lawyer, Adam Chernok. "It's arguable it would have been a much more difficult case to prove and indeed may not have obtained the plea of Lindholm."

Chernok added that while Lindholm had a "primary motive" to kill her lover, his client's only motive was "put very simply, your honour, sex."

"If the killing of Amey is Lindholm's wicked design, it is not a truly shared motive in terms of the killing as I've described," Chernok said. "My client is motivated by sex in the context of his particular circumstances."

David Hallowes, who defended Ryan, claimed his client didn't become involved in the plot until after he'd been told that Amey was "mistreating" Lindholm. According to Hallowes, Ryan had believed the plan was only to "beat" Amey – and that without Lindholm's participation, the murder would never have happened.

However, according to Justice Philip Priest, the two men had ample opportunity to back out of the plan while Amey was still alive in the trunk of the car. The fact that they continued with the murder shows "how nasty this killing was."

"Lindholm sought to bring about Amey's murder for two years," stated the judgment from the Court of Appeal in October of 2016, dismissing the bid from the trio. "She tried to persuade others to kill him for her, and eventually, she persuaded Trabert to do it. Trabert and Ryan callously, ruthlessly, and violently carried out her wishes."

In fact, the statement added that Lindholm had continued to arrange for Amey's murder even after she'd broken into his apartment and received a community corrections order. According to court records, Lindholm and others had conducted surveillance on Amey, and she'd broken into the apartment even though she had a swipe card that could have been used to gain entry.

Records show she had told an associate that she'd done this so that "if something happened in the future, it would look like she did not have access to the property."

"It is difficult to overstate Lindholm's moral culpability for this crime," the court said. "She pleaded guilty but the (sentencing) judge found that she was not remorseful. In our view, the sentence imposed on her was a merciful one in the circumstances."

More than sex on legs

Supporting the charges were a series of text messages exchanged between Lindholm and Amey in the weeks leading up to his murder, included as part of the police evidence against Lindholm.

"Look at that ring on your finger Rob," read one message from Amey to Lindholm. "The one I designed, had made and ask you to marry me with, AND I MEANT IT. What better chance could anyone get? You cheated on that ring and me. Remember that when it's on your finger next time you sleep with him."

"Wayne you wouldn't take me back. I tried for months," said one of Lindholm's texts to Amey. "After I recognized my mistakes you still rejected me. I was only good enough to f—k. That was all. When I f—-ked up I was in a bad place lonely and messed up. I know that hurt and I don't know why I did it but the last few months when I begged to come home and I wanted you more than anything you still rejected me continuously. And took everything away."

"I need to feel like I'm more than just sex on legs," she said. "There's Robyn here too not just Collette."

Another text from Amey stated that Lindholm had gotten herself "in this position from a LIFETIME of lies, deception, drug abuse, selfishness and hate."And in another message to Amey, Lindholm told him that if he made her life any more difficult than he already had, "you will regret it Wayne."

According to Lindholm, the couple had been drifting apart for years. By the time their relationship started, Lindholm was in her 30s – ready to get married and start a family. Amey, though, already had a son from a previous relationship and decided to get a vasectomy. According to Amey, the couple "couldn't afford" a child because of their outstanding debts.

By 2009, Lindholm was even more frustrated with her relationship with Amey. He'd promised to retire with her at the Bittern property following his 50th birthday – but that never happened.

"She anticipated that the pair of them would live out there and she would raise her horses out there and they would see out their twilight years together there," said Kelly, Lindholm's lawyer.

Officially, the pair split in 2011, but according to Lindholm, Amey continued to reach out to her for casual sex, right up until his death.

"He was very into that and whenever he got drunk or smashed he used to call me and that was right up until not long ago," Lindholm told police after Amey was killed. "We used to do a lot of threesomes and he used to get me to bring girls home a lot."

However, despite what Ryan had been told about Amey "mistreating" Lindholm, she told police their relationship had never been violent. In fact, she claimed Amey was "kind" to her.

"We loved each other, but we just grew apart," she said. "I would never let anyone hurt (Amey) because he's never hurt me. He was always good to me."

An average guy

According to Amey's teammates from the Camberwell Hockey Club, he was happy, friendly guy – who happened to get in with a "fast crowd." While he wasn't known for sharing many details about his personal life, he had broached the topic of his relationship with Lindholm about three week before he was killed.

Amey had felt as though a weight had been lifted from his shoulders, believing that his dispute with Lindholm over the Bittern property was coming to an end – it was finally on the market, and once the property sold, Amey would be able to get a brand-new start.

"He spoke openly about a breakup some time ago that had turned sour and threatening," said Dugald Jellie, a teammate from the hockey club. "(Amey) was caught in a drama he couldn't undo. He'd tried restraining orders. He wanted only to quit his ex-partner and her friends, sell his country retreat, then one day sell his gym and start anew."

As a youth, Amey had been a top-grade hockey player. As an adult, he'd taken to playing in Camberwell's veteran's squad and working with the club to help develop its younger players. Jellie was one of his hockey mates, who had traveled with Amey to a game in Geelong just a few weeks before he was murdered. He was deeply affected by the news of Amey's death.

"It frightens me to think of (Amey) being hurt and in such peril. It is awful to think of him being so vulnerable, so helpless, so in need of his friends when none of us were there," Jellie said. "I can't stop but think of the moment he was jumped, and of his fears, and how alone he must have felt."

Active investigation

While serving her 25-year sentence for arranging Amey's murder, Lindholm received a new set of charges in June 2016 – naming her responsible for the murder of George Teazis, back in 2005. Appearing before the Melbourne Magistrate's Court via video link from the notorious Dame Phyllis Frost Centre women's prison, Lindholm refused to enter a plea, or speak at all, other than to confirm her name to the magistrate.

In 2017, defence counsel will hold a committal hearing and plan to cross-examine more than 20 witnesses, which will determine if Lindholm will then stand trial.

Investigations are ongoing to determine the extent of Lindholm's possible involvement in the disappearance of Shari Davison, as well.

KILLER SEDUCTRESS

GARY RACE

Shayna Hubers

Shayna Hubers is a 21-year-old graduate from Lexington, Kentucky. She grew up in a comfortably middle-class family and was a smart young woman. She graduated from Paul Laurence Dunbar High School in 2009, and went on to college. During high school, Shayna's friends described her as quiet and "most likely to succeed". Shayna graduated from Kentucky's prestigious School of the Arts after making Dean's list in 2012. She was in the process of pursuing a Master's Degree in counseling from Eastern Kentucky University when she took the life of her on-again off-again boyfriend, Ryan Poston and effectively put her life on hold.

Poston was a 29-year-old lawyer and business owner from a successful family of attorneys and executives. He was loved by his friends and family and admired by women. He was known to be friendly, respectful and respectable, and an overall good guy. He met Hubers in 2011 through mutual friends on Facebook and the attraction was instantaneous, as the first photos of Hubers that Poston saw were racy in nature. The two began to chat, and started officially dating shortly after they went on their first date. They continued their relationship for over a year. If it hadn't been for Facebook, the two more than likely never would have met, as Shayna lived 80 miles away from Ryan and had no reason to venture into Ryan's neck of the woods.

Throughout the entirety of the relationship, the couple sent thousands of text messages, including a conversation about possibly taking a two-week long break from each other and the relationship. Hubers was also known to post pictures of herself and Poston on Instagram. The seemingly happy couple exchanged over a thousand photo messages, as well as 20,000 messages through Facebook. Most of the Facebook messages had been sent by Hubers to Poston, who had responded to only a handful of them.

To people who weren't aware of the couple's dynamics, it appeared as if they were a happy couple who had everything going for them. They were both beautiful, successful, and driven. It was a match made in heaven- or so it appeared to be, but the truth was much darker and would become the subject of a complicated trial and a life term in prison.

On October 11, 2012, Hubers and Poston and his family had dinner at the young lawyer's home. After dinner, Hubers went home- she returned a few hours later, however, and the couple got into a heated argument. Poston informed his girlfriend that he wanted to end their 18-month long relationship, and it set Hubers off into a fit of anger. Her anger worsened when she was later told that Poston already had a date lined up with the 2012 Miss Ohio, Audrey Bolte. It's believed that the news of Ryan's new date was what pushed Hubers over the edge.

In the morning, Hubers' mother drove two hours to pick up her daughter and the two went out shopping. They were out for most of the day before Shayna was dropped back off at Ryan's house, telling her mother that she wanted to stay with him. Despite her other asking her numerous times to come home with her, Hubers was adamant that she wanted to stay at Poston's house. Shortly after, Poston became aware that Shayna was planning to stay at his place- he used this time to inform her that he had another date and didn't intend to spend the night with her. By 9 o'clock that night, the young lawyer was dead on his dining room floor.

At 8:53 that chilly Friday night, Hubers placed a 911 call from Poston's condo and said to the responding dispatcher: "Ma'am, I have…I have…I have killed my boyfriend in self-defense".

The dispatcher then asked what happened, to which Hubers replied "He beat me and tried to carry me out of the house and I came back in to get my stuff. He was right in front of me and reached down to grab the gun. I grabbed it out of his hands and pulled the trigger".

The dispatcher then instructed Hubers to step outside with her hands in front of her. Hubers complied, and responding officer, David Fornash's partner cuffed and took her away while Fornash himself went to investigate the crime scene.

Fornash and the other officers who responded to the scene, found Ryan Poston lying on his dining room floor next to a Sig Sauer .380-caliber pistol. The pistol, upon further inspection, was found to have belonged to Poston, who had a passion for guns. "…he would have them in his boot, he would have them in his holster…" says Poston's ex-girlfriend, Lauren Whorley, who claimed that Poston's love of guns made her feel safe.

Fornash went room to room, double checking that there were no other hiding in the apartment and upon finding Poston's body, officers found that he had been shot once in the back, twice in the head, and three times in his upper body. The coroner is called and Fornash sets off for the station where Hubers had been escorted into an interrogation room and sat waiting.

Meanwhile Poston, lying dead on his kitchen floor, was supposed to meet with Audrey Bolte at the Milford Inn bar for a night of drinks and harmless flirting. Poston, however, did not show up and Bolte went home feeling confused. When asked how she felt about him not showing up, Bolte said that it was odd for Poston not to show up or give some sort of notice that he wasn't coming, as he was a very responsible individual.

Friends of Poston claim that he and Hubers were never really in a committed relationship, as Poston lost interest in Hubers rather quickly and made several halfhearted attempts to break it off with her. In fact, by October of 2012, Ryan had made 3 attempts to sever Shayna's ties to him. According to text messages between Poston and his cousin, he was emotionally drained from dealing with Shayna. "I received 75 text messages from her. I am emotionally and mentally spent. I hope she leaves me alone" reads one message between the cousins. Despite this, Poston continued to go out with Hubers and pose for photos.

Shayna, confiding in a friend through text messages, said that Poston had told her that he's only with her because he felt bad when she cries. She is also quoted as saying: "My love has turned to hate."

In one particularly chilling message Shayna claims that "...tonight when I go to the shooting range with Ryan, I want to turn around, shoot, and kill him, and play like it's an accident." The next day, Shayna posts a photo of herself with a gun at the shooting range.

The night of the murder, Shayna was interviewed about the incident. Left alone in the interogation room, Shayne almost seemed proud of what she had done, reports Chief Bill Birkenhauer. He watched her on live camera snapping her fingers, dancing around, and muttering to herself "I killed him, I killed him."

Legally, officers were not allowed to interrogate her without an attorney present, so when she was brought into the interview room they didn't ask any questions. In fact, officers didn't say anything. Shayna, however, readily volunteered her story of how the events took place. She was rambling on for two hours before running out of things to say. According to officers, the men and women who took turns sitting with Shayna, quickly grew tired of her rambling and would have preferred to leave. "Shayna appeared to be nervous, or trying to cover something up" one officer said. "...her stories, after a while, stopped matching up and kept changing." This, according to the officer, might have been happening as a result of Shayna realizing that she was in over her head.

When speaking about Poston's death, Hubers said that she knew he was dead because he was twitching. Her exact words were: "Literally, that's when I knew that he was dead or close to it...the twitching...and that was it." She goes on to explain how she couldn't let him sit there and twitch. She couldn't stand to sit there and watch him die so she shot 5 more rounds into his body to finish him off.

In addition to building a case of self-defense and trying to convince officers that she deeply loved Ryan, she claims that "he was very vain...he wants to get a nose job...I shot him right here-" she pointed to her nose and continued her story "...and I gave him the nose job that he wanted."

Officers didn't buy Shayna's claims of self defense due to lack of evidence that Poston was ever abusive towards her. "She claimed that she was pushed and that he hit her, however, there were no visible marks or wounds at all on any part of Shayna's body" says former FBI profiler James Fitzgerald.

"There was no evidence in Ryan's condo that there was a fight" adds Laura Richards, a prominent criminal behavioral analyst.

Photos from the crime scene show evidence against Shayna's claims of a fight, as there were a number of pill bottles and bullets standing on end on the table. Had a fight taken place, they would have been knocked over or displaced and the murder area would have been left a mess. Instead, it was neat and tidy other than the pool of Ryan's blood that was left behind after the shooting. Shayna had also claimed that Poston had thrown her against a bookshelf. The bookshelf in question, when police arrived, was undisturbed.

As for Shayna's odd behavior when left alone, Richards believes that it was an act in an attempt to appear mentally unstable and open the door for the insanity plea should her self-defense claims fall short. "She couldn't decide which plea to go with- self-defense or insanity. So, she decided to open the doors to both and see which one panned out the best."

After three hours of deliberation, Shayna is charged with one count of first degree murder. In 2014, her trial is well underway and a forensic pathologist mentions that at the time he was shot, Poston had been sitting down- a fact that goes against what Shayna had said previously. According to Richards, this fact alone blows Shayna's claims of self-defense out the window as it shows that Ryan was not charging at her in a fit of rage, as she had previously claimed. Instead, he had been seated and had been seated great distance away from Shayna at the time of the murder. Forensic expert Howard Ryan backs this theory up by going into detail about the shots that Shayna fired at Poston. He says that the first shot was to Poston's head, a fact that is significant due to the lack of blood found on Ryan's shirt.

"If he had been standing up, the gravity would have brought it down...straight down the shirt through the bottom to the pants" he says.

Using the blood stains on the table, Ryan is able to provide further detail as to why he believes that Poston was sitting down. "When she shoots him in the forehead, his head goes down on the table." Poston's head would not have fallen onto the table if he had been in an upright position. From here, Ryan suspects that Poston's back was left exposed, setting him up for the next shot. At the same time that he is being shot a second time, his right arms falls limp and opens up the area of his body that will receive the third shot- which is right underneath of his arm. After this, his body slumps to the floor and remains there until it is removed by the coroner.

Three of Shayna's cellmates testified against her that day, claiming that she had told them that she intended to kill Ryan that night and that he had never been abusive to her. "She laughed about shooting him in the face and giving him the nose job he always wanted" claims Cecily Miller.

Another inmate, Holly Nivens, claims that Shayna made the whole abuse story up. When speaking about the bruises and scratches that Shayna would show people, Nivens claimed that Shayna inflicted them on herself.

Shayna also told her cellmates that she had messed the apartment up and thrown objects around to make it appear as though a vicious fight had taken place.

Shayna didn't take the stand, but prosecutors used her social media and interview footage as a substitution. Despite the overwhelming evidence against Hubers, her defense team maintained its argument that Poston had been abusive and that Shayna had acted out of self defense when she shot him.

A toxicologist was asked to plead in Shayna's defense and said that at the time of his death, Ryan had a strong mix of Xanax and Adderall in his system. He argues that these medications could have caused outbursts of anger and violence, making it possible for Ryan to snap and come after Hubers with a both his fists and then later on, a deadly weapon such as a gun.

A clinical psychologist was also called to testify on her behalf, and he diagnosed her with bipolar disorder with narcissistic tenancies, and post traumatic stress disorder (PTSD).

"She was very distraught. She was depressed" says the psychologist who claims that Shayna had told him that she had suffered from sexual abuse as a child, and was recognized as having alcohol and prescription drug abuse issues.

On the day of the trial, Shayna painted herself as a model girl friend to Poston, claiming that he had been going through a lot and that she had always been there for moral support.

"I was always good to him" she said.

Again, the jury didn't buy the story. Five hours after her trial started, Shayna was officially charged. She appeared back in court three months later for sentencing and was given 40 years behind bars. Shayna's defense team tried to lower the time before she becomes eligible for parole to 8 years instead of 20, but was denied this motion.

Just six months later, her legal team filed another motion seeking a new trial. According to her team, one of the jurors who convicted Shayna had not been legally eligible to convict her as he was a convicted felon himself. This, according to Kentucky law, made him unable to serve the court and gave Shayna's legal team a reason for a new trial.

It's said that Shayna's new trial date is set for early 2018. Until then, she is behind bars and serving her 40 year sentence as planned.

The new trial was originally set for January of 2018, but has been put on hold for 4 months longer at the request of Shayna's legal team. The extra time, according to her attorney, will be used to prepare.

Despite the 40 year sentence, Ryan's friends and loved ones are left with a sour taste in their mouths. Lauren Whorley, in an interview with a news station, claims that she wishes she would have known what was going on- maybe then she would have been able to help and prevent Ryan from getting too tangled up in Hubers. She also said that she believes the trial should have been handled in an "an eye for an eye" fashion, meaning that what Shayna did to Ryan, should have been done back to her as justice.

"Maybe it's traditional, old-school mentality, but if you kill someone, then you know, it's an eye for an eye. And what you due unto others should be done unto you" she said.

For her, however, the sentencing brought a sliver of much appreciated peace. "I was there when they read it" she said about the final verdict "It was the longest 30 seconds of my life."

Matt Herren, a close friend of Ryan, still struggles to make sense of what went wrong that night. "I think about him everyday," he says "You just don't think something like that will happen to someone you know."

Like Whorley, Matt wonders if there is something he could have done to prevent Ryan from suffering the fate he did. "I know a lot of people in his life feel the same way" he says to "48 Hours" correspondent Peter Van Sant.

Van Sant asked Herren what was lost when Ryan was killed and Herren responded with "He's the type of person you want in your life. Not just a friend, but a loving son, a protective, older brother. He had three younger sisters that he adored." Poston had cared deeply for his three younger sisters and only ever wanted the best for them. In return, they showered him with love and looked up to their older brother.

Ryan and his family had been close-knit, despite his mom and dad divorcing when he was a child. He was close to his father, and when his mother remarried, he grew an attachment to his new step-father, Peter Carter. Ryan thought of him as a second father.

According to Sarah Robinson, a woman who had grown up with Shayna, her future had seemed promising as well. Shayna had been a good student and was never in any trouble.

"I thought she was, close to genius, in my opinion" she said " I mean, she was always in AP classes. Always getting A's in everything."

During her academic career, Hubers had received various awards for academic excellence and leadership.

"She liked to succeed at anything and everything she did" Robinson concludes.

When Van Sant asked her what Shayna had been like with boys in high school, Robinson mentioned that Shayna could be dramatic. "If a guy, broke up with her or something, she would take it pretty hard" she explained "...crying, and a maybe a bit of screaming..she didn't really like to let things go."

When asked if Shayna had been happy with Ryan, Robinson said that as far as she knew, she had been. As far as she knew, they had both been happy.

Ryan's friend, Allie Wagner, claimed that there was something wrong with the relationship from the start when she was asked the same question about Ryan. According to Wagner, Shayna had been cold upon their first meeting. "You could just immediately tell that...that she was obsessed with him," she says.

"He was busy with work..he didn't really have time for anyone" Herren adds. "He didn't want to hurt her feelings..that wasn't the kind of person he was."

As Shayna's denial towards Ryan's disinterest progressed, he started to wonder if he might need to put a restraining order out against her. "This is getting to be restraining order level crazy..." he wrote in a text message to his cousin "She's shown up at my condo 3 times and refuses to leave each time."

Ryan's neighbor, Nikki Carnes claims that there may have been two sides to the tumultuous relationship. She says that Ryan may have been emotionally abusive. According to Carnes, Shayna complained frequently of Ryan putting her down. "She told me that he would say she needed a boob job or a face lift and that she was fat and needed to lose some weight" she says.

Van Sant then asked her why Shayna wouldn't have left and she replied "I guess because she was young and she always told me she loved him." Carnes also told Van Sant that Shayna did everything for Ryan from taking his dog outside to picking up and doing his laundry. On the night of the shooting, she also reportedly heard gunshots but didn't hear the couple fighting, as Shayna had claimed that they had.

Wagner, when asked what she thought could have happened that night replied, "I think she went over there...tried to talk him out of breaking up with her. And I think he just stood his ground for the first time," she said "I think he just said no, like, this isn't working. So she picked up the gun and shot him."

Chief Birkenhauer agreed with Wagner's theory "He wanted to break up with her...I think that Shayna was not gonna be broken up with" he said in an interview with Van Sant.

Prosecutor Michelle Snodgrass explains why Shayna's pleas of abuse were dismissed. "Someone who is in shock does not pirouette," she says in response to the police videos of Shayna singing and dancing in the interview room "Within hours of putting six bullets in Ryan Poston and watching him die, she was dancing and singing."

"There were hundreds of thousands of text messages. And most of them were from Shayna. For every 1 message Ryan sent, she sent probably 50," Snodgrass says "She couldn't stop herself."

According to Snodgrass, rejection was what ultimately pushed Shayna over the edge and drove her to kill the man she so desperately loved.

"Ryan's a bright guy; he's a lawyer" says Van Sant to Snodgrass "Why wouldn't he get a restraining order?"

"Under the law in Kentucky, he didn't qualify for a restraining order. The law in Kentucky required the two to have been living together or to have been married" she replied.

Van Sant then spoke to Hubers' mother, Sharon, about the tragedy. "She graduated cum laude in three years at the University of Kentucky. She was pursuing a Master's Degree in school guidance counseling," she said.

"And what do you want people to know after reading this" Van Sant asked "...in relation to this case?"

"Shayna Hubers is not a child, a girl, a person that would murder someone; that would wake up and say 'OK, I'm going to shoot somebody"

"I want the world to know who Shayna is. And I want them to hear it from her mother" she concludes tearfully.

Hubers and her mother had been close most of Shayna's life, according to Sarah Robinson. "I think she was very close to her mom. I think her mom, for a good portion of her life, could have been her best friend."

This statement is backed up by a quote from Sharon Hubers in her interview with Van Sant: "That child has been a blessing to me. She's my whole life."

"The word that has been used to describe your daughter is evil" Van Sant teold Sharon.

"She's far from evil. Shayna has a heart of gold. She's like her mommy...a loving spirit. That's what I want the world to know" she replied.

After the trial, Shayna spoke up for the first time. Despite having killed their beloved family member, she didn't apologize to Poston's family. Instead, she apologized to her family and friends, and speaks only of herself.

"I'm sorry to my family. And I'm sorry to my friends for letting them down. And I'm sorry for the money my parents had to spend on attorneys" she says, after being convicted of the murder.

"I do wanna help people. I do wanna be something better. And I do want to continue to grow and learn" she said to the judge "And I just don't think a 40 year sentence will help me. I don't think it would benefit me any."

Judge Fred Stine replied to Shayna's statement with his own choice words. "What I think happened in that apartment was little more than cold-blooded murder."

Regardless of what happened that night, a promising young lawyer lays dead, and a successful college student sits rotting behind bars. Two families have been destroyed, and law officials are left baffled. Both the victim and offender have been robbed of their lives- and for what? For a reason that the offender calls love.

Killer Seductress : Pamela Smart

Sarah Thompson

The case of Pamela Smart is infamous and retold in popular media through episodes on crime-based drama. What is it about Pamela Smart and her affair with a fifteen-year-old boy that draws society to continue to retell her case? The murder of Gregory Smart, Pamela's husband, is one that tells a story not often seen in the trends of women who commit murder.

Women who kill are so statistically and socially interesting to us that we, as a society, often gather up their specific stories into anthologies and special documentaries. Television shows like "Snapped" and "Deadly Women" focus exclusively on female cases of murder. Meanwhile, television shows that have been going on since the early nineties, like "Forensics Files", have an overwhelming number of male offenders. Of course, this isn't to say that women are incapable of murder, or that they do so infrequently. In fact, statistics have proved that women are entirely capable of killing, and often do so.

Information gathered by the Bureau of Justice Statistics, with data gathered between 1976 and 1997, shows the rate of murder committed by females was about 1.3 per 100,000. That is to say, for every 77,000 women, one would end up to be a murderer. The victims, in this case, were overwhelmingly the spouse. 60,000 murders were committed by women between the years of 1976 and 1997, and 60% of the victims were an intimate partner or family member.

While these numbers may be shocking, the context of the killings is also important. For example, 92% of all women in California prisons are estimated to have been battered or abused by either the spouse, intimate partner, or family member at some point in their lives. In 1992, data gathered by the Georgia Department of Corrections showed that of the 235 women that were currently serving time for either murder or manslaughter, 44% of those women had killed either their husband or intimate partner. However, of those women who had revealed that they had killed their spouse, 96% of them also admitted to having suffered domestic violence in the relationship.

Overwhelmingly, the reason that women kill is to escape a relationship with an abusive partner. With this knowledge, the next question is: what of the women who kill without the thought of self-defense in mind? What are the reasons and motives of the women who kill their perfectly loving and agreeable spouses? The women who kill in self-defense can be empathized with. But there is still a seedy underside to female murderers, the ones who manipulate the people around them and use others to their advantage to do away with their spouses. Not all women kill directly, after all. Some women manipulate others to do the deed for them.

The story of Pamela Ann Smart began in 1967. She was born as Pamela Wojas, on August 6th, in Coral Gables, Florida. A middle child, Pamela grew up as the second of three children. Her sister, Elizabeth, was six years her senior while her brother, John, was three years her junior. The children were born to a father who worked as a commercial airline pilot and a mother who was a part-time legal secretary. Her home life was good, and she went through childhood unmarred by violence or abuse by either her siblings or her parents. During her elementary school days, Pamela and her family moved from Florida to Windham, New Hampshire. There, Pamela flourished. She attended high school at Pinkerton Academy in Derry. She became a cheerleader, and her high school days floated by, still untouched by any particular violence or trauma. She was popular, and while she had a strained relationship with her father, she was very close to her mother.

After high school, Pamela decided to return to Florida for college. She attended the Florida State University and during her time there, Pamela worked on the radio, where she hosted a once a week show at WVFS. The show had a theme of heavy metal music, which Pamela loved. She called the show "Metal Madness", and her radio personality was under the alias of "Maiden of Metal". Pamela had a love for both heavy metal music and radio. After all, she was getting her degree in communications. Combining these two loves seemed like the only logical choice. It was during her time in college that Pamela met Gregory Smart. The year was 1986, and they were both at a New Year's Eve party. Pamela and Greg hit it off right away. Their relationship was intense from the beginning, and the two were seriously connected by February of 1987.

In 1988, Pamela graduated with honors and a degree in communications. Pamela was a smart and studious woman. Her academic achievements were nothing to be looked down upon. She achieved her degree in just over 3 years at the Florida State University, while maintaining a 3.85 grade point average. A year after her graduation, in 1989, Pamela and Gregory finally married, and Pamela went from Wojas to Smart. The marriage began as most marriages do, with a honeymoon phase that lasted only a short while. But while it lasted, the two were absolutely devoted to one another. They settled down in their hometown of Derry in New Hampshire, with a beautiful home on a quiet, residential street. Greg even bought Pamela a Shih Tzu, which she named 'Halen' after her favorite heavy metal group, Van Halen. Married young, Pamela was only 23 and Greg was absolutely devoted to her. They were the all American couple. Greg was excited about the start of his new life, with his perfect wife. His family recalls him talking at length about how Pamela would become a wonderful mother, so certain of his new wife's caretaking abilities.

Pamela, perhaps, was not as eager to begin life as a mother. She often described herself as a "typical Leo". That is to say, she always desired to be the center of attention. She had always been popular, even in high school, and she carried that bubbling charisma with her everywhere she went. While she was outgoing, loud and boisterous in her personality, Pamela was also needed to be in control: of herself and her surroundings, including the people in them. Her clothes were always nearly coordinated by color, and she lived by a very strict schedule that didn't allow much room for disruption. When her self-imposed schedule was thrown off, Pamela would become upset. Despite their fundamental differences, Pamela and Greg had a happy marriage - for a short time.

It was only 7 months into the marriage before the happiness the two shared started to waver. Their relationship went from blissful happiness to having serious issues. It's no surprise that the honeymoon phase of any relationship would begin to fade, but after only seven months Pamela and Greg's relationship was facing challenges. While Pamela longed to continue their rock and roll image, Greg began to grow up more quickly not long after their marriage. He cut his long blonde hair that Pamela had first fallen for, which was only the beginning of Greg's new, conservative attitude. He took up a job at the same company that his own father worked at. He traded in his intense love for heavy metal, which had first brought him and Pamela together, for the ambition that it took to become an accomplished salesman.

Pamela and Greg were simply growing apart as people, perhaps having married each other at too young of an age.

It was nearing their first year anniversary when Greg finally admitted to Pamela that he was having an affair. From then on, Pamela admitted, that her trust had been broken. She didn't feel important to her husband anymore. Her own interest in the marriage began to wane. After the admittance of the affair, Pamela's interests had turned into her career. After all, the graduated early with an astounding grade point average. Her desire to pursue a broadcasting career had not diminished in the slightest. Greg was unaware that Pamela wanted out of the marriage after the problem with the affair arose. Although she brought it up during every argument, talk of separation never came up.

Pamela, with her unhappy marriage and desire for freedom, took up a job at Winnacunnet High School in Hampton, New Hampshire, as a communications director. While it wasn't the glamorous job in broadcasting that she was hoping for, Pamela believed that it was a step in the right direction. Her duties included producing and distributing educational videos to the school districts. It wasn't quite the same as her heyday as the Metal Mistress back in college, but she was granted both her own secretary and student intern. In addition to this, Pamela also volunteered at the local drug awareness program, Project Self-Esteem, as an adult facilitator. She made a big impression on the freshman who were expected to participate in the program. All of the freshman students at Winnacunnet High School enjoyed Pamela - she was young, pretty and she could relate to them through a shared interested in heavy metal music.

Pamela got along well with the freshman who participated in the program. She was never patronizing and was young enough that she and the kids shared a lot of the same vernacular. She even wowed them with stories of her time in the heavy metal scene and her wild times backstage at concerts.

It was at Project Self Esteem that Pamela Smart met Billy Flynn. Their ill-fated meeting would change the course of both of their lives for good.

William "Billy" Flynn and Pamela Smart met in the fall of 1989. He was 15 years old, and one of the teenagers that worked on Project Self-Esteem. He was smitten with her right from the beginning, and would often go out of his way to help her. He even made routine visits to her office after the meetings. Billy Flynn shared Pamela's love for rock music. He was attractive and still growing into his looks, with blonde hair down to his shoulders - the same hairstyle that Pamela had loved in her own husband, and lamented it's lost. Despite his age, Pamela wasn't much older than most of the kids that she spent her days around, and it was easy for her to get lost in their acceptance. Around the same time that Pamela and Billy met, she was also reeling from her husband's admitted affair.

It was no surprise that Billy Flynn got caught up with Pamela. He was born just one day after an explosive argument between his parents and was always caught in the middle of their rocky relationship. He grew up watching his father mistreat his mother through anger and overbearing control. As the first child, it wasn't long until Billy was also the subject of his father's anger, and continued to experience it even after his siblings were born. Billy's father was reportedly a great man when things were going his way, but once that stopped his anger got the best of him and he would start yelling and berating whoever was within earshot. This put a strain on Billy and his relationship with his father.

Finally, spurred by his father having an affair, Billy's parents divorced. Soon after, Billy and his brothers moved with their mother from California to New Hampshire. It was here that Billy, young, angry, and suffering the trauma of a divorce, would meet Pamela, and change the course of his entire life.

Pamela's affair with Billy Flynn began when he was just 15. Pamela had become overly friendly with another one of the students under her charge, Cecelia Pierce, who was the student intern assigned to her at her position as a communications director. Pamela and Cecelia were like best friends, and Pamela showered her with attention. Because of their age differences, Pamela most likely made Cecelia feel important. After all, she was only 15 and Pamela was 23, an interesting adult who wanted to hang out with her and treated her like an intimate friend. Pamela's friendship with Cecelia soon began to show signs of being controlling, just as her "Leo" personality would suggest. The more time she spent with Pamela, the more her grades began to slip.

Pamela, Cecelia, and Billy would hang out like teenagers. While Gregory was out of the house, Pamela would invite the two teens over to watch movies or work on video projects together. It was during one of these times that Pamela and Billy first engaged in sexual intercourse. The time of the year was near the end of March, and Pamela had invited both Cecelia and Billy over to watch movies while her husband was out of state for a business meeting. After one of the movies ended, Cecelia went outside to walk Halen, the beloved Shih Tzu. While she was gone, Pamela brought Billy up to her bedroom, where she put on a piece of lingerie that she had bought specifically to seduce Billy Flynn. It was there, while their friend was out walking the dog, that the two had sex for the first time, in Pamela and Gregory's marriage bed.

Despite all the things she and the teenagers had in common, it's hard to understand why a grown woman would choose a 15-year-old as her lover - unless, of course, Pamela had other plans in mind for the needy and impressionable Billy Flynn. The morning after their first time together, Pamela said to Billy: "Last night was great, but we can't keep on like that." When Billy questioned why, Pamela said, "Because of Greg. If you want to keep seeing me, you'll have to get rid of my husband."

And just like that, the seed of Pamela's plan was planted. All that was left was to help it grow into a murderous, poisonous plant. Despite her conviction that they couldn't keep seeing one another, Pamela continued to engage in her relationship with Billy over the course of the next few weeks. Each time, she would continue to complain about the looming threat that her husband posed to their budding relationship. She even confided in Billy that Greg would beat her—although, this wasn't true. She continued to threaten that they couldn't keep seeing one another unless her husband was gone. Pamela explained to Billy that she couldn't get a divorce because her husband was too controlling. She told the young man that she would lose the condo and her dog. Billy, who had no reason to distrust his friend, teacher, and lover, believed the lies that she fed him. He was hopelessly in love, and it was then that the plans began to solidify.

Billy Flynn agreed with kill Pamela's husband. She had manipulated this outcome by repeatedly holding her affection and relationship hostage from him, with Gregory Smart as the threat that would tear them apart. Billy Flynn, just 15 years old and without the constitution of a murderer, flaked out on two attempts at Gregory's life. Each time, Pamela would berate him, threatening to leave him. While Billy couldn't yet see it, Pamela's motivations were clear: she was using her position of authority and her sexuality to manipulate Billy Flynn into committing the murder that she so desperately longed to commit, but refused to risk getting caught for. There was no star-crossed love between them, an angry husband keeping them apart. Pamela knew that she could manipulate a lonely, starry-eyed boy into disposing of her husband, and it wouldn't matter what happened to him after that.

Billy Flynn, faced with the threat of being left by the woman that he considered his lover, knew that he would have to start thinking seriously about killing Gregory Smart. He would later tell the jury that he thought Pamela would leave him if he chickened out of the murder one more time. Billy started confiding in his two friends, J.R and Pete, who had been in Billy's circle since he moved to New Hampshire from California. The three boys began plotting, with Pamela as encouragement. She gave them a deadline of May 1st, and promised the boys a cut of the insurance money that she would later collect.

While the boys were planning their attempt on Gregory's life, Pamela and her husband's marriage was falling into further disarray. Of course, this would be no surprise. After all, Gregory was living with a woman who was actively planning to kill him. There was no love left between them, and the strains of the marriage continued. They fought often and argued over the pettiest things. Gregory would come home to an empty house, and the couple would not see each other for days on end. Regardless of Pamela's desire to see him dead, the marriage was clearly ending. The two young lovers had simply grown apart. Where Gregory had grown into a businessman with responsibilities, Pamela had decided to stay surrounded by teenagers and relive her youth a while longer.

Finally, the plan to dispose of Gregory Smart was coming together. Unsurprising to anyone, it was Pamela who gave the boys primary directions. Pamela would leave her backdoor and cellar open. Billy, J.R, and Pete would enter the house and begin to tear it apart, making it look as if a robbery had taken place. She even instructed them to take electronics, jewelry and anything valuable to make it seem real. The lights were to stay off, as Pamela insisted that if her husband saw any of the lights on, he wouldn't come inside. She also didn't want the dog to be hurt, and so she instructed the boys to stick Halen in the basement so he wouldn't be traumatized by witnessing the murder of one of his owners. Finally, Pam insisted that they use a knife rather than a gun because she didn't want blood all over the apartment.

The plan would conclude with Pamela coming home to discover her husband, ostensibly murdered during a vicious robbery attempt.

May 1st, 1990, was the day that the plan would take place. That morning, Pamela got up and acted as if it were any other day and not the very last day of her husband's life. She exchanged morning pleasantries with her husband as they went about their morning routines. She tended to Halen and the two had breakfast together before they parted ways. Pamela must have been hyper aware of what was going on, and what would happen, while she watched her husband go about his day without any knowledge that it was his last. After all, most people never know which day is their last.

Gregory left for work before Pamela, who then headed out the door around 9:45 that morning. She had plans that would keep her busy all day and give her the alibi she needed to get away with conducting and orchestrating her husband's murder. She was attending a school board meeting that planned to go later than usual due to a salary review. Attending this meeting would ensure that Pamela wouldn't return home until after night had fallen - until Gregory was dead. Around 2:30 in the afternoon, Pamela and Billy met by his locker to discuss a small hiccup in their plan: they needed a ride to go pick up the getaway car, which belonged to J.R's grandmother. Perhaps leaving three teenage boys to do the dirty work is dispatching her husband wasn't the smartest idea that Pamela had, but it was all she had to work with. All the same, Pamela drove one of the boys out to get the car, and the rest of the plan was back in action.

Just before 8:30 pm, Billy, J.R, Pete and a fourth boy, named Raymond Fowler, commenced with the plan. Raymond was a boy often on the periphery of the group. His role in the plan was minor. Billy and Pete entered the condo while the other boys waited outside in the courtyard. While the ransacked the house, Billy tossed Halen into the basement - the dog, reportedly, fell down the stairs while the other boys laughed. After the dog was locked downstairs, they continued on with the plan that Pamela had set out for them. They took jewelry and took apart the electronics to make it look like a real robbery. After they had done their duty messing up the condo, Billy Flynn and Pete waited in the darkness for Gregory Smart to return home from his day, entirely unaware that they would be waiting for him.

Despite Pamela's insistence that they use a knife because of the mess, J.R had taken a gun from his father's collection and given it to Billy. The boys waited in the darkness by the backdoor, ready to jump Gregory the moment that he entered. When he did, it was Billy who leaped first, out of the darkness and onto Gregory. Pamela's husband was immediately overtaken by Billy and Pete. They stole his wedding ring to complete the robbery-gone-wrong image.

Finally, Billy said: "God forgive me," as he pulled the trigger just inches from Gregory Smart's head, and the man dropped dead to the floor.

The plan was completed. The boys escaped the condo, and their friends were waiting with the getaway car. They made their way back home. Billy had completed the task that Pamela had set out for him to do. He had killed her husband, in the anticipation that they would finally be able to be together. In the aftermath that followed, it was Pamela's job to play the grieving widow. According to the detective who worked on the case, Daniel Pelletier, she wasn't as good of an actress as she thought. Her interview with Detective Pelletier raised all kinds of concerns. Pelletier said, "From day one, she wasn't acting the grieving widow." Unfortunately, that was her only job in the plan she had concocted.

It was Pamela who insisted on an interview with the detective, and during that time Pelletier continued noticing strange things about her story. She described stepping over the body and noticing the speakers on the stand. She described the scene as a "botched robbery", rather than focusing on the death of her husband. The final thing that tipped Pelletier off, however, was when he took Pamela back to the condo to gather things she needed before closing it off as a crime scene: Pamela walked over the blood stain where her husband had died. Not around it: over it, multiple times until it was covered with a towel.

On May 2nd, just a day after the murder, detectives were already discussing the idea that it was Pamela who had done it, not yet aware of her influence on four teenage boys. It took two weeks before an anonymous tip led the detectives in the right direction: Cecelia Pierce. Detectives also got information from a boy named Ralph Welch, who had overheard J.R and Pete discussing their roles the homicide. While the detectives couldn't get the boys to talk, Cecelia finally told them everything. She agreed to be wired and tape a conversation between herself and Pamela in order to get the evidence that they needed. Pamela was convinced that it was her word against the boys and that she was home free, despite that word was getting around about her own involvement. It was Cecelia who managed to get Pamela's confession on tape, acknowledging that she knew that the murder was set to take place before it happened. That was all the police needed to set the rest of their plan into action to put Pamela away for good.

On August 1st, 1990, Pelletier arrested Pamela Smart for first-degree murder. Police Captain Jackson was on the scene as well, and had this to say of Pamela: "She thought she was smart, but she had no street smarts. [...] That was the problem. She that she was smarter than the whole world. But she made many mistakes, right and left."

The trial lasted only 14 days, and the main argument was about whether or not Pamela Smart had control of Billy Flynn and the other boys enough to make them murder her husband, or whether those boys did it on their own. Pamela continually insisted that she had no prior knowledge, and that she had lied to Cecelia on the tapes received of their phone calls. Pamela admitted to the affair with Billy Flynn, but refused to admit to prior knowledge of the planned murder. Her testimony consisted of confessions of love for the teenager. When it was Billy Flynn's turn to take the stand, he described everything: from Pamela's insistence that he kill her husband, to the night of the murder.

"I cocked the hammer back and pointed the gun at his head. I stood there for a hundred years, it seemed like," Billy Flynn said in his testimony. And while the court argued back and forth whether or not

Pamela had controlled Billy to do what he had done, it was clear why he had done it.

On March 22nd, 1991, the jury deliberated for all of 13 hours before they came back with a verdict: guilty. Pamela was sentenced to life without parole on the charge of accomplice to first-degree murder. A follow-up hearing sentences her with conspiracy to commit first-degree murder and witness tampering. New York State, where she still remains to this day serving her life sentence.

As for the boys, Billy Flynn and Pete are serving their time at the Maine State Prison in Warren, Maine. The fourth boy, Raymond Fowler, was paroled in 2003, sent back after violating the terms, but released again in 2005. J.R was given a 30-year sentence that was then reduced by 12 years to 18, and he was paroled in 2005. Cecelia Pierce, on the other hand, came out on top, having signed away the rights to her story of the case for $100,000.

Pamela Smart is an interesting case when it comes to women who kill. After all, she didn't lay a hand on her husband. However, she abused the influence that she had on her impressionable students and managed to use a combination of sex and power and to manipulate a young boy into committing a crime that he could never take back, and one that would never have crossed his mind had Pamela not been the one to put it there. So, despite the fact that she wasn't even in the house while her husband was killed, Pamela Smart still goes down in history as one of the most infamous "women who kill".

AMNESIAC KILLER : THE TRUE STORY OF DANIELLE STEWART

LES ACKERMAN

"I would punish all of those who had never lost anything, those who had never had anything taken away from them. I would let the anger from my chest reach out and explode in spectacular violence." - An excerpt from a poem by Danielle Stewart

Danielle Stewart had a normal and happy childhood until around the age of seven. Both of her parents were public servants and the family lived in the Curtin, Canberra region of Australia. She had one younger sister and the family seemed en route to living a normal, happy life.

Danielle was particularly close to her father during her childhood years. He took her swimming, read books to her at night and sang to her. She described him as being a man with a great sense of humor and the kind of man who "did all the things that dads do."

At the age of seven, however, Danielle's life took a traumatic turn. Her family was building a holiday house in the NSW south coast town of Batemans Bay. Danielle, unfortunately, came into the cross hairs of a sexual predator.

The man was a neighbor and Danielle would come over to his home to watch TV as they had no television of their own in their holiday house. The man was a married real estate agent in his 50s. He would let Danielle and a friend come with him to outings where they would examine unoccupied houses he was selling. It was there, inside these homes, that the assaults would take place.

Danielle would be under the man's spell for over three years before they molestations came to an end.

When she was eleven years old, tragedy struck again in the form of losing her mother to cancer. Distraught, her father sent her away for a weekend with a friend of a family. The family had a teenaged son, however, who constantly harassed Danielle, molesting her as well.

Her father would remarry six months later to a woman who had three children of her own. Danielle felt betrayed by her father's remarriage and tried to commit suicide with an overdose of pills. Her father himself had suffered from depression and fell apart emotionally after the death of Danielle's mother.

"I've always believed that depression and mental illness is inheritable," forensic psychologist Pauline Malloy said. "Sometimes through genetics, sometimes through thought processes. With Danielle, she clearly inherited some mental illness from her father's side of the family as her dad suffered from depression as well as her paternal grandfather."

Her maternal grandparents arrived and offered that Danielle come live with them. Danielle didn't want to go, she wanted to stay with her Dad but her father didn't want her screwing up the dynamics of his new family with her bad behavior.

He wanted her gone.

So Danielle was given two choices, either go live with her grandparents or go to a youth shelter.

Danielle chose to run away

"Danielle suffered numerous traumas, back to back," Malloy said. "The loss of her innocence, the loss of her mom and then the rejection of her father. Any of the above could have been cause for life altering psychological trauma but she suffered all of these within a four year time span. It had to crush her psychically and she did not have the life experience to cope."

Running away, the twelve year old girl roughed it out on the streets. Finally, she grew tired and returned home to her father. She would not be treated as the prodigal daughter, however, as her father had her bags packed and waiting. He drove Danielle to a local youth shelter and dropped her off.

Danielle would remain there for the next three months.

Danielle did not like the youth refuge. There was a lot of drug use, alcohol and she once again experienced sexual abuse.

"This was a horrid life for her at this point," Malloy said. "At some point I think she broke down psychologically and the seeds for future violent behavior were planted here."

RETURNING HOME

She eventually returned home to live with her father but he had settled in with his new family.

"I felt so alone, unloved, misunderstood," Danielle recalled. "and as the problems at home got worse, I got worse. I was sneaking out of the house, drinking, drugging. I missed my mum so terribly, I just wanted to be with her."

Danielle would attempt suicide on several occasions, leaving permanent scars on her wrist.

"I used a razor in my bedroom downstairs," Danielle said. "There was no internet back then and I didn't know how to do it [properly]."

On her 13th birthday, her father celebrated by throwing her out of the house once again. She would go and live with her friend Elle O'Brien and her mother. O'Brien's mother fed her and took her in, allowing the unwanted girl to remain there for four years.

At the age of sixteen, she enrolled at Narrabundah College and become a student of renowned poet Geoff Page.

"She was leagues ahead of anyone I've encountered writing contemporary poetry at that age," Page recalled. "She had some of the same virtues as Sylvia Plath, a real feeling for adventurous imagery. There was a lot going on in her brain at an intense level and she had the talent to turn it into something moving."

Under the guidance of her teacher, Danielle published an anthology of poems called "I for Icarus."

Danielle would go on to study performing arts at Melbourne's Monash University before traveling to Sydney to share an apartment with her step-sister, Myfanwy Thompson. Both young women would indulge in alcohol and prescription drugs, becoming the catalyst for each others self-destructive behavior. Myfanwy, however, would suffer a freak accident in falling off a cliff while taking ecstasy.

The loss devastated Danielle as she considered Myfanwy to be her best friend.

"Her boyfriend had got into dealing ecstasy," Danielle said. "I couldn't handle seeing her wasted all the time, so I'd moved out with other friends."

Her younger step-brother, Tristram would later die of an aneurysm after being diagnosed with schizophrenia.

MEANDERING THROUGH LIFE

Danielle was now 24 and wandered aimlessly through life. She went from one job to the next until she met the 50-year old Chaim Kimel in late 2000.

"They met on the dance floor and hit it off immediately," journalist Byron Kaye said.

Despite the age difference, Chaim Kamel was a stylish man with his own business.

"He was a bit of a bon vivant," crime author Paul Kidd said. "Lived in the good part of Sydney. A good lifestyle."

"He was very charismatic, very gregarious, very charming, very generous, strong and creative," Danielle said. "He loved his children and they loved him."

Kimel had been a successful entrepreneur, dealing in antiques. She got a job working for Chaim in his furniture store, Eclectica in Mosman. Kimel had put Danielle in charge of bookkeeping.

The two got along exceptionally well, at first, with common interests in art, music, and food.

"Danielle was a very attractive," Kidd said. "Petite, blonde, loved to drink. He (Chaim) was an older man but a really good style of a bloke."

The relationship started platonic in the beginning.

"He made some advances which weren't initially reciprocated," Kaye said. "But over time, they became intimate and it was on."

Kimel thought Danielle was a "prize catch". He invited Danielle over to visit his family and she was impressed with how close and living they were. There she saw, for the first time since her early childhood, a loving family that she could be a part of.

Danielle moved in with Kimel who had the time lived with his ten year old son Jordan. He also had a daughter, Amber and Fred, who were in their early twenties and late teens respectively.

A CHANGE IN DEMEANOR?

One of her friends, however, thought that Danielle changed after she met Chaim. She described him as being very possessive and told her what to do.

"I loved him," Danielle said. "I still do. It is a love-hate thing and it won't ever go. With those types of personalities, there is that level of attention, you become their entire focus."

Danielle would have these kind of intense relationships all of her life and it seemed to be the fuel to her fire. She was irresistibly drawn to the drama and would have it on full blast with Chaim Kimel.

"Anyone who would have been in a relationship with Danielle Stewart would have been in a relationship that was doomed from the start," Kidd said. "The combination of psychological problems fueled by excesses of alcohol was always going to end in disaster."

COCAINE AND BOOZE

Danielle began substance abuse at an early age which only progressed as she got older. She now had a benefactor in Chaim as well as an enabler as he liked to party, indulging in cocaine himself.. He didn't realize, however, that the alcohol would only stoke the flames that would extinguish their relationship.

He also had a dark side, according to Danielle's grandmother. She described him as someone who was "demanding and overpowering."

"She (Danielle) went through life with a paranoia that people were going to leave her," Kidd said. "And she became very, very possessive of her partner and that fueled by alcohol was the basis of the majority of their problems."

CALL THE POLICE

Once the relationship turned intimate, things started getting out of hand. The two indulged in alcohol and had numerous fights in which the police were called in.

Danielle had been taking strong anti-depression medications and mixing these drugs with alcohol. One fight had gotten so severe that she took a restraining order out against Kimel.

On one occasion, Kimel violated the order and was jailed for one night.

"I'd moved into temporary accommodation and Chaim came after me," Danielle said. "He broke into my room and stole my laptop and wallet. The police busted him on the way out and took him to jail for the night."

Kimel explained to the police that he violated the order because Danielle had called him stating that she had swallowed fourteen Valiums.

"I'm fine when I'm not in an emotional situation," Danielle said, "but when I'm under threat, the flashbacks can be extreme."

"She (Danielle) had a borderline personality disorder," Malloy said. "When things go bad with her, they go real bad. That was how she lived her entire life up until that point. She had to engage in fights, drinking, drugs. Drama, drama, drama. If it isn't there, she will create it."

A PROPENSITY FOR VIOLENCE

Kimel's son, Jordan, was ten years old when his father first met Danielle. He recalled Danielle as a destructive psychotic stating that she would "cut up $10,000 worth of business suits, delete important documents from my father's computer. Once, she punched through a glass bathroom window and slashed her wrists. And she'd punch my father, too."

"Unfortunately, this was the pattern that was set," Malloy set. "They would argue, fight and then get back together. When they would get back together things would be more passionate and clingy than before. 'Please, don't leave me,' that sort of thing. But then the cycle repeats itself and it has to be more extreme in order for the couple to get that same 'high.'"

The couple would remain together and make attempts to appear respectable. In 2004, Danielle enrolled at a nearby college to finish her degree while they both started an online catering company called Epicurean. The money to start the company was borrowed from Danielle's grandmother, a total of $30,000.

Later that year, the couple would journey to India where they would marry at the Taj Mahal.

Danielle would claim, however, that the money the borrowed for the business is what kept her in the marriage .

"Part of the reason I married Chaim was because I was worried about my grandparents' money," Danielle said. "If I left him, there'd be no legal recourse for me to get it back. He took it without shame; he never planned to pay it back."

"Typical of people with borderline personality disorders," Malloy said. "Is that they have to play the role of the victim. It is a head scratcher as to why Chaim would borrow thirty-grand when he had his own business. Maybe he thought he would be placating her somehow with them being in business together and having her feel as if she were a part of things. But clearly he didn't need anything more on his plate."

BOOMERANG BABY

Danielle would leave Kimel a total of seven times during their seven year relationship. She would confide in her grandmother and friend Elle, saying she was unhappy. Then he would call and they would get back together.

"It (their relationship) was very alcohol fueled," Kaye said. "Very hedonistic. A lot of violent arguments."

Danielle blamed her inability to stay away from Chaim on her lack of self-esteem.

"While he could be caring, it was undermined by his desire to keep me enslaved to him," Danielle said. "When I left him, he'd follow me and get me back. When your sense of self-esteem is so low and a learnt helplessness has set in, you don't feel able to support yourself. My friends had dropped off because they couldn't stand him. The only times I responded with violence were when I was trying to leave and he'd try to stop me. He'd hide my wallet, phone, computer, passport. Those times always ended with me being in hospital, not him. I never tried to kill him: I tried to kill myself."

WHO WAS ABUSING WHO?

It became apparent to Kimel's family, however, that he had married a woman prone to violent outbursts. Kimel told his daughter than Danielle had bitten him on his thumb and arm as as smashing his glasses.

He had his glasses broken so much that it had become a "running joke", according to his daughter Amber.

After arguments, Danielle would delete Kimel's emails and computer files. Kimel had became so enraged at her actions that he kicked her out of the house. Danielle would return, kicking out the timber door.

WELCOME TO THE PSYCH WARD

Danielle had overdosed on medication numerous times during the course of her marriage. She would inform doctors that Kimel was controlling and that she had "nothing to live for."

His daughter, Amber, however, expressed concern for her father's well being and wanted him to sever ties with Danielle.

"He told me he'd made a commitment to be there for her and loved her unconditionally," Amber said. "He was convinced unconditional love would cure her."

"Chaim was the rescuer," Malloy said. "He couldn't help himself. Danielle was the beautiful damsel in distress. They had passionate sex together, he knew about her past, and he couldn't be another man that brought more pain in her life. He didn't want that. He thought that through his own sincerity and love that he could somehow bring her to a place of healing. But he wasn't a professional. And that isn't what relationships are for."

A NEW MAN

In 2006, Danielle separated from Kimel and met Melbourne university professor Joeri Mol. She moved in with him and became pregnant by December of that year. Danielle wanted to go back to Sydney, however, and didn't want to raise the child with Mol as a single mother.

"She went out with somebody else," Kaye said. "He was seeing other people but they could not stop speaking. They remained extremely close. The new fellow (Mol) wants to settle down and start raising a family. Which incidentally was Danielle's greatest dream, which was to have a family. But she's still drawn to Chaim uncontrollably."

A week later, she called Kimel and the two met to discuss a reconciliation.

"He (Chaim) told her that either she as a termination," Kidd said. "Or there's no hope if them ever getting back together."

She complied with his request, her second abortion in six months (the first with Kimel) and she once again went into a depression.

"Danielle desperately wanted to experience the happiness that she had before her mother died," Malloy said. "She always told her grandmother, 'I just want have a normal life. I just want to have a normal life.' What she really wanted was that family again. So now she spends her life grasping at straws, going from this man to that man, and getting multiple abortions."

BURNING THE CANDLE AT BOTH ENDS

The couple moved back in together in 2007 but this time their break-up would be much more volatile.

And violent.

"It was short lived (their reconciliation)," Kidd said. "Now that they were back together. It was business as usual."

Business as usual was a lot of fighting and alcohol coupled with a flurry of activity to keep up with the bills.

Danielle returned to college and continued to run their catering business, The Epicurean. In order to make ends meet, however, she took a part time job at a Sydney ad agency.

She couldn't juggle all of these things at once, so she turned to cocaine and alcohol. Her friends described her as "withdrawn" and "unsettled" after meeting with her after the latest reconciliation.

Danielle began to feel the itch to run away again, telling friends she now just wanted to earn some money on her own and get away from Kimel for good.

"How the hell could this have worked to begin with?" Malloy said. "You've got a woman with some serious issues, abused by men, abandoned as a child and now she's an alcoholic with major depression. The pattern is set in their relationship. Break-up, get back together, fight some more. Rinse and repeat. This can only end badly. The question was, how bad?"

THE FATEFUL DINNER

"The old problems kept resurfacing," Kaye said. "They kept on with the dinner parties. Living the good life. And with this came Danielle's terrible response to alcohol access."

On August 23rd of 2007, Danielle went out with Kimel to have dinner at a restaurant called Pescador. They were described in a police statement by their friend, Angela Batley, to be in "good spirits."

"It is noted by others there that Danielle seemed a little drunker than usual," Kaye said. "Things got a little bit more testy and Danielle left and decided to walk home."

After dinner, Chaim went with his friends to Angela Batley's home. He would call Danielle from the home and she said that she would come and pick him up. Things took a turn for the strange when Danielle came over but drove back without Chaim who ended up walking home.

Batley was concerned about the tenseness of the situation and called Kimel to make sure he got home safe. Kimel told Batley that Danielle was working on the computer but was "drunk" and that he had to go.

Danielle arrived at their home before Kimel. She told the 16-year old Jordan that she "shouldn't have gone to Angela's house. I've had too much to drink."

Jordan stated that Danielle began playing loud music through the computer, dancing with a drink in her hand. When Kimel arrived, he told her to turn the music down before the neighbors start complaining. An argument ensued before Kimel turned off Danielle's music himself. The argument escalated, the topics being the loud music then escalating to the fact that Chaim would change the password on the computer, which was an ongoing issue in their relationship.

She started to physically attack him but Chaim easily evaded the rushes of the drunk Danielle. Then in the heat of the moment, she picked up one of Chaim's antique ornamental knives he had on display. Chaim came forward, ordering her to place the knife down, then she stuck it into his stomach.

Chaim fell to the ground and she stabbed him again.

"They were both yelling for about 15 minutes," stated Jordan. "All of a sudden, I could hear them in the corridor outside my room. It sounded like someone was being hit or punched and I heard my father say, 'Why are you being violent and attacking me?' They kept fighting and I heard Danielle fall to the floor and scream. Soon after this, I heard my father say in a tense voice, 'What are you doing? Are you crazy?' I heard my father scream three times. I saw [his] white shirt was covered in blood all up the left side from underneath his ribs towards the middle of his torso. Danielle was standing about two metres away and she had our antique knife in her hand."

Jordan saw his father struggling to get to the front door. He was covered in blood and Danielle was hysterical, holding up the knife.

"So the son runs out of his room," Kaye said. "He finds his father clutching his stomach where he's been stabbed twice. Covered in blood. Barely able to speak."

Jordan then thought about attacking Danielle himself.

"He picks up a golf club then thinks for a moment, that he might avenge his father," Kaye said. "It's actually Chaim himself who tells him don't do it. Lying there, sort of holding himself together. The son puts the golf club down and nurses his father while he lies there dying."

Kimel would be rushed to the hospital but die on the operating table at St. Vincent's Hospital, bleeding to death from the two stab wounds to his stomach.

"To the end of his life," Malloy said. "Kimel was protecting Danielle. When his son wanted revenge, he held him back."

Danielle was arrested but plead not guilty on the grounds of self defense. Her blood alcohol reading, however, was five times the legal driving limit.

"It was a stupid, pointless, uncontrolled lover's argument," Kaye said. "And one split second decision led to this terrible outcome."

Danielle maintained no recollection of the events, as she mixed the anti-psychotic drug Seroquel with alcohol. She awoke in a prison cell and called out for her husband, seeing her name on the board with the word 'Murder' written next to it.

"It was the worst moment of my life," Danielle recalled. "In one instant, my entire life had changed and Chaim's had ended."

"Something was going to happen that night," Malloy said. "Her mind was on edge. This may not have been pre-meditated but she knew what was going to happen when she picked up that knife. Remember, she didn't just slash at him as a warning. She thrust the knife into Chaim. Not once. But twice. There was an untapped rage there that came to the surface at the moment. It had been bubbling for a long, long time and unfortunately Chaim Kimel could not foresee how this would end."

THE AFTERMATH

Danielle made a recorded phone call to her father a few days after the killing.

"If I could swap Chaim with me right now, I would do it immediately," Danielle said. "There is no way I meant to kill him."

"Again, I don't think the murder was pre-planned," Malloy said. "But it did seem to be part of Danielle's destiny. What we see here in her killing of Chaim was a metaphor of her own trauma. She was abused by a man in his fifties, molested by him from the ages of seven through ten. She grows into a beautiful woman can choose just about whatever man she wants but instead she elects a man in his fifties, over twenty-five years her senior. That is no coincidence. She is repeating her trauma from the past. But this time she wants to control it. She wants to exorcise the demons of the past so all of those violent fights are trial runs until finally she reaches for that knife and stabs Chaim, metaphorically killing the molester of her past. Now her husband, who actually really loved her, is the victim of this cycle of abuse that has finally come full circle."

Her father agreed to post Danielle's bail but would not agree to the 24-hour surveillance condition attached to it. Her father abandoning her yet again, she turned to her friend Elle O'Brien's mother. She came to bail out Danielle and secured her release after nine months.

Danielle then went to live with her grandmother.

Facing twenty-five years in prison, Danielle would attempt suicide two more times, one of them involving an overdose of Seroquel.

"When I took that Seroquel, I went into psychosis," Danielle said. "It was an out-of-body experience where I thought the nurses were talking about me even though they weren't. I was watching myself from afar. It was crazy, crazy shit. I am sure that is what must have happened on the night Chaim died."

"The psych med plus alcohol defense has become a cliched defense for a lot of killers," Malloy said. "Danielle had done her research. She had studied scriptwriting in school. Everything she said and did had a rehearsed feel to it."

FROM MURDER TO MANSLAUGHTER

The murder charge had been downgraded to manslaughter as Danielle maintained she had no recollection of what happened. She did not remember any of the events of what happened that night not to mention taking the ornamental knife and stabbing her husband with it.

She did not take the stand, however.

"Danielle was charged with murder," Kaye said. "She wept throughout much of the trial. It was very clear that she regretted what she'd done and she wanted him back and she felt quite horrible."

Kimel's children, however, saw Danielle as an imposter the more they investigated the case. They found a synopsis of a play that Danielle had been working on. In the story, one of the characters had a secret desire to kill her older husband.

Fred Kimel, Chaim's oldest son, noted that the play contained details on "jail architecture, prisoner psychology, different cell classifications, prisoner attire, prison visiting hours and life sentences."

The Kimel family once enamored with Danielle, now saw her in a completely different light.

"It was a university assignment, a book I was writing," Danielle said. "I heard that somewhere men kill their partners because they want them to stay, whereas women kill their partners because they want to escape. I know why I was writing about prison: because I was imprisoned long before I was [actually] incarcerated."

SENTENCING

Danielle would be sentenced to six years in prison. She would serve only four.

"There's no doubt that jail saved me," Danielle said. "It prevented me from harming myself with alcohol and drugs. I wouldn't recommend it, though."

During the first nine months of her term, she had been housed in the mental health unit. She could not stop crying. But the prison assigned her to a job in the kitchen and she found her fellow inmates to be helpful.

"I managed to get a few of the heavies on side somehow and avoided the others where possible," Danielle said. "I learnt to assimilate, to hide the fact that I was pretty and educated. I adapted where I could. In jail, I lost everything that made me me: my family, dog, business, house, studies, friends, freedom, clothes, make-up, choices. All I had was myself, my mind and my heart. I learnt to spot evil from a mile away - and evil does exist, I've come face to face with it - but I could still love. This is how I got through jail. Yes, I learnt how to operate within the system, but I could still see beauty in people, and I tried to speak to that."

"Danielle was a well-spoken, educated young woman," Malloy said. "But why the hell would she plead not guilty? She did her research on prison culture beforehand so a cynic can argue that she got off very, very light for what she did. Call it misandry, call it getting the female pass, Danielle was able to get off light for a cold-blooded murderer. She used all of the things from her past to mitigate her own culpability. Sexual abuse, parental death and abandonment down to psych meds and alcohol. She combined those things to get sympathy from Chaim and later from the her jury of her crime."

Danielle walked out of prison on June 24th, 2010.

She is now focused on the prospect of moving to Spain and becoming a professional writer.

"I've paid for what has happened and I've done all I can to fix the issues within myself that contributed to Chaim's death," Danielle said. "I see both a psychiatrist and a psychologist, both of my own volition, nothing to do with parole directives. I don't drink. I don't take drugs. I take responsibility for my actions. I write when I can. I try to love my friends and family. I try to see beauty in the world and I'd like to hope, one day, that I can contribute to that beauty. Still, I love. I still love Chaim. I still love my father. In the end, love will be all I have."

SHE KILLED THE PREACHER

John Fontaine

The Case of Mary Winkler

Mary Winkler, at first appearances, would seem to be an altogether normal woman. So too did her family, with a husband who was a Church minister and three young children, girls aged just eight, six and one.

The family lived in Selmer, Tenn., a small town occupied by around 4,500 people, according to the 2015 census. The town is situated to the south west of the state. Not much has happened in Selmer; the most famous person to have been born there was Chad Harville, former pitcher for the Oakland A's, and for one year, the Red Sox. He achieved a 4-9 win-loss record over his career in the MLB.

Today, the most famous- or infamous- person to have come from Selmer is Mary Winkler. In 2006, Mary sparked a border-crossing manhunt, and a court case followed nationwide. She had killed her husband with a shot to the back from the family's shotgun. But it was the gripping, and at times bizarre, court case which gripped the attention of the nation.

Matthew dead, Mary and the family Missing

The date was March 6th, 2007. It was a Tuesday like any other. Mary and Matthew were at home all day together, although Matthew was due to give a sermon that evening.

It was actually members of Matthew's congregation who found his body that night. They had visited his home to check up on him after he had missed the service he was set to give; instead, they found him lying dead, having been shot in the back.

There was no sign of Mary or any of their children at the home, and as such, they were reported missing. The authorities quickly sent out an Amber Alert, since nobody had any idea what could have happened to them, or where they might be. Family and friends had no information to provide police on their whereabouts.

There was every chance that the family had been kidnapped or murdered, and their bodies disposed of elsewhere, although police could not identify a break in, and had no reason to believe that anything of value had been stolen.

It was only a day later that she was arrested in Alabama, having run from the family home with her young children. They were found 350 miles away from home, at Orange Beach, and in the back seat of the van was the family's shotgun. It was certainly suspicious; but what reason could Mary have possibly had for committing such a crime?

The Trial

In the build up to the case going to trial, public interest ramped up. Speculation had been rife about why Mary would have murdered her husband, a seemingly nice, well respected member of the local community. Perhaps either one of them had had an affair, and Matthew had been killed in a crime of passion. Or maybe he had been killed for an insurance claim?

As such, the press reported every step of the story as it came out during the hearing. The trial began when a Tennessee Bureau of Investigation Agent John Mehr read a statement that Mary had made very soon after her arrest. In it, Mary claimed that the couple had been arguing about their family finances, before Mary had shot her husband with their 12 gauge shotgun. She had said that the last thing she had wanted was to actually murder her husband, but she had been brandishing the gun in an effort to convince him to work through their problems, together. The argument had been ongoing throughout the day, and Mary had finally snapped, resorting to drastic measures to be able to convince him. She had never intended to kill him: she had said in the statement, 'I don't want this at all. I don't want any of this to be, at all.'

The statement continued on, and Mary claimed that they had argued often and argued fiercely. 'He had really been on me lately,' Mary had said, 'criticizing me for things- the way I walk, I eat, everything. It was just building up to a point. I was tired of it. I guess I got to a point and snapped.'

At first glance, it would seem that Mary had simply lost her composure, become angry, and killed her husband 'as the red mist had descended'. But after their initial statement, Mary's attorney indicated that there was much more that would come out about Matthew's behaviour when she testified which would help to explain her actions. Clearly, there were more problems with their marriage than the occasional, albeit fierce, argument.

Mary's Crime

The case for the prosecution wasted no time in painting Mary as a cold blooded killer, who left her husband to die without remorse. Admittedly, the plain facts of the case made Mary seem unbelievably guilty. The prosecution relied on several of these facts in their attempt to convince the jury of Mary's guilt for the charge of murder.

Mary had disconnected the phone immediately after she shot her husband, stopping him from being able to call the emergency services, or receive any calls that may have come in. This suggested that Mary had been in full control of her actions, not panicking, since it is unlikely that somebody in a state of anxiety would think to disconnect the phone.

The fact that Mary had attempted to flee to Orange Beach, Alabama, was also a key point for the prosecution. Immediately after Matthew's death, Mary had taken the family minivan to the beach, with her three children. Later on in her defence, Mary would claim that she ran because '[n]obody would believe me, and they'd take the girls away and put me away.' Certainly, in many murder cases, the fact that the defendant flees the scene is a certain indicator of guilt.

The family's daughter Patricia testified that she couldn't understand her mother's actions. All that she knew was that she had heard a 'big boom', and the sound of something heavy hitting the floor. She quickly ran to the bedroom to see her father on the floor, and her mother holding the shotgun. She had no idea what could possibly have provoked her mother to shoot him.

Another sticking point was that the family finances had been 'in shambles' just before the murder had taken place. This had led Mary to become embroiled in what is called a 'check kiting' scam. In it, she had received checks from unidentified accounts in Canada and Nigeria, and had ultimately fallen to a financial scam that had lost the family money. Prosecutors claimed that this could have somehow instigated the argument that led to Matthew's death, and that Mary had felt as if she had no way out of the scam.

They also jumped on the fact that in an initial conversation with investigators, Mary had told them that their marriage was a happy one, and that '[t]here's no poor me. I'm in control.' They clearly wanted to paint a picture of Mary as remorseless, deceitful, and smarter than she looked.

The Cross-examination

During her cross-examination in court, Mary stated that she didn't remember grabbing the gun from the closet in which it was kept. What she did remember was that 'something went off', 'hearing a loud boom', and that 'it wasn't as loud as I thought it would be.' She did admit that she had shot her husband. Matthew rolled from the bed- upon which he had been lying as they had argued- and dropped to the floor. Mary described smelling gunpowder.

Prosecutor Walter Freeland asked her whether she understood that 'pulling a trigger is what makes it go boom', to which she replied that she did.

Matthew asked her why she had snapped and shot him. She could only say 'I'm sorry.' The shotgun blast had been inflicted from behind, directly into Matthew's back, and had caused severe damage to his organs and spine. According to prosecutors, he had in fact still been alive as Mary had run from the house.

But these simple facts were far from the end of the story, as Mary was to reveal.

Appearances and Revelations

At first, Mary spoke of her husband not in the past tense, but in the present, as if she couldn't quite understand how final her actions really had been. In reminiscing about happier times, Mary told the court that her husband was an intelligent, social man, and that the family had shared many 'good times' together. She also seemed to enjoy talking about her children, and the happiness they brought her.

This happy family life, however, was simply one side of the marriage. Mary's attorney stated that '[w]hat went on behind their closed doors is going to have to be told ... Some of what we've got from the state of Tennessee touches on sexual abuse.' Their defence was that Matthew had made Mary's life a 'living hell': '[w]e will show you proof that he would destroy objects that she loved, he would isolate her from her family and he would abuse her not just verbally, not just emotional and not just physically—in other ways, too.'

Just before the murder, Mary claimed that Matthew had been threatening their children and even attempted to throttle their infant daughter, Breanna. He had been shouting, angry, because he had wanted a son. As the case went on, it became obvious that this was only the tip of the iceberg, however, and more and more sordid details of their home life would come to light.

Matthew, Mary claimed, was a violent, abusive husband. Shortly after their marriage, he ordered her to stop socialising with any of her family and friends (a common tactic among abusive spouses in order to further isolate their partners from potential help). Winkler's sisters described how Mary seemed stuck in her marriage, unhappy, but unable to leave. In an interview, they said that 'As the years went on, she seemed to be nervous to show love towards us.'

Mary was commonly 'screamed and hollered' at by her husband. 'He just flailed. He's a big guy and he was just all over ... He'd point his finger inches away from my nose. Whatever he was upset about, it was my fault,' Mary had said. It could be over anything: 'I was fat, my hair wasn't right, the girls, if something went wrong, it was my fault. I didn't know when it was coming.' Mary described her situation as one familiar to abused wives and husbands across America.

Her attorney, Steve Farese, provided further information based on his conversations with Mary. She had needed her husband's permission for everything, even for getting her hair cut. 'This was constant, and she lived a life where she walked on eggshells.' This abuse, he said, had given Mary symptoms of post traumatic stress disorder, simply because 'she didn't know what was going to happen next.' Furthermore, a psychologist testified as part of Mary's defence, saying that her symptoms were those of clinical depression and PTSD.

During her time on the stand, Mary also claimed that Matthew had forced her to watch pornography with him, and that he had bought her several 'slutty' costumes for sex, which she normally would never have worn, but for fear of her husband. If she refused, Matthew wouldn't hesitate to get physical, hitting her or even using his belt to whip her. Mary famously produced a wig and a pair of white high heels in the witness box during her cross-examination to show the court evidence of Matthew's other side.

Mary stated that she was never happy watching pornography, dressing up in sexy outfits or performing the sex acts that Matthew wanted. She went along with his ideas, however, because she didn't dare face his reaction if she didn't. 'I'd just do anything to help him stay happy.' Throughout these revelations, Mary was visibly embarrassed and uncomfortable. Clearly she would have preferred that none of them had ever come to light; but Mary felt it necessary to brave what her neighbors, and the nation, might think in order to clear her name and justify her actions.

Mary's family had been quick to corroborate her side of the story. Her father, Clark Freeman, had spoken out through Good Morning America and detailed the 'physical, mental, verbal' abuse that his daughter had suffered. Other friends came forward during the court case, and gave similar verdicts on their relationship. A friend of Mary's, Rudie Thomsen, said that '[o]ne Sunday, Mary came into the church and I looked at her and she had a black eye.' Similarly, Mary's friend Amy Redmon agreed that Matthew had been controlling: '[h]e was an authority figure, and he made the decisions basically. It was obvious.'

Conversely, Matthew's family denied that their son had been anything like Mary had depicted in her defence testimony. Matthew's father, Charles Daniel Winkler, said that his son was a kind, gentle man, who could have done nothing to justify what the defence was claiming. Diane spoke several times during the trial, lashing out at Mary: 'You've never told your girls you're sorry! Don't you think you at least owe them that?'

The dramatic story of a supposedly kindly, gentle church minister having such a sordid, cruel and abusive hidden life gripped America. The case was covered extensively on all major networks, discussed on late night panel shows

The Jury's Verdict

While the prosecutors had tried to convince the jury to convict her on a charge of first degree murder, they were unsuccessful. The jury came to their verdict by April, that year. It took them eight hours to deliberate their way to the decision; this mirrored the response of the nation, which was similarly undecided on just what punishment Mary really deserved.

Mary was found guilty of voluntary manslaughter, a charge which carries a far more lenient sentence than murder. While murderers can receive full life sentences, and in certain states receive the death penalty, the maximum sentence for voluntary manslaughter is only 6 years.

Mary showed little emotion at the verdict, but did embrace each of her relatives afterwards. In a show of support, her family had been sat in the row behind her, and all linked arms with one another to demonstrate their solidarity. Afterwards, she was taken back into custody to await sentencing.

Mary's attorney stated afterwards that Mary's testimony had been central in securing the more lenient sentence. 'I think Mary's testimony was integral in this decision. They had to hear it from Mary', Farese told the press. 'They judged her credibility and they saw that she had an abusive relationship and they made their judgment based upon that.'

For Mary, the most important implication of the verdict was that she could finally begin to think of being reunited with her children. Speaking on her behalf after the trial, Farese continued: 'We would like to do so many things to open up communication between Mary and the paternal grandparents and to get the children out of this cycle of constant upheaval over this terrible tragic event.' But the question of how long she would be in prison remained.

Mary's sentencing was scheduled for May 18th, at which point both Mary and the prosecution would have a final chance to address the court before the judge decided on the final jail term. However, the situation looked positive for Mary. Not only would the five months that she had been imprisoned awaiting trial be taken into consideration, but the judge had indicated that alternatives to incarceration would be on the table. Perhaps Mary could avoid jail time altogether.

Sentencing: The Trial at an End

Due to a scheduling error, the hearing took place around three weeks late, on June 8th.

Mary took to the stand one last time to plead for mercy. She read aloud from a prepared statement, telling Matthew's family of her sorrow and remorse for her actions. She was 'so sorry that this had happened', and would 'always miss and love' her husband. 'I ask for mercy and understanding, but I know whatever decision you reach today will be right ... I ask you to please let me go home today and be with my children.' Tabitha Freeman- Mary's sister- had also pleaded for leniency, in particular to let Mary be reunited with her children. She went as far as calling Mary 'the best example of a good person I can think of'.

Members of Matthew's family, too, took to the stand to plead their case for the prosecution. Charles and his wife were clearly hurt and in disbelief at Mary's actions both in murdering their son, and believed that Mary had purposefully smeared his name at trial. 'The monster that you have painted for the world to see? I don't think that monster existed,' Diane Winkler had said.

After speaking their pieces, all that Mary, her family, and Matthew's parents could do was wait until the judge's decision. The trial- as well as the very public 'trial' that Mary had been through in the media- was finally at an end.

The defence had requested that Mary be granted full probation, or judicial diversion, both outcomes which would have meant that Mary would spent no further time in prison, and even that her record would be cleared of wrongdoing altogether. This request was denied.

After recess, Mary was told that she would spend 3 years in prison for her crime. But Circuit Judge J. Weber McCraw reduced that amount to just 210 days total in prison before she would be allowed to leave on probation. She also had that sentence reduced further, due to the fact that she had spent five months incarcerated waiting for trial.

Moreover, that time would be spent not in jail, but in a mental health centre in Tennessee. There, she would receive treatment for both her depression and post traumatic stress disorder. After such a long ordeal, with the prosecution fighting to either put Mary on death row or to imprison her indefinitely, it seemed that she had gotten off with hardly a slap on the wrist.

Steve Farese branded the sentence 'a victory': '[s]he could be in prison for life, and that's what everybody thought she was headed for to begin with.' Her other attorney, Leslie Ballin, said '[s]he'll be able to get out and fight the battle she wants to, and that is to get her children back.' Mary could finally think about the future again.

But certain signs indicated that it would not be as easy to reconcile with her children and family as she might hope. Matthew's family left the courtroom without making a comment to the press, as did the prosecution, clearly disappointed in the verdict. They gave no indication that they would be happy to open dialogue about Mary's daughters- not with the woman whom they believed to have murdered their son in cold blood.

The aftermath of Mary's release

Mary was released on August 14th, 2007. She had only been sentenced the previous June.

Upon her release, her lawyer informed the press that Mary would not be speaking with them, to maintain her privacy. During her time in the mental health facility, Mary could finally begin her attempt to win full custody of her three daughters, and she was still fighting this case at the time of her release. She had not seen her children, apart from Patricia's brief testimony as part of the case, for over a year. Throughout the case, and after Mary's release, her children were staying with Matthew's family.

Moreover, she was still fighting a \$2 million dollar civil lawsuit filed by Matthew's parents. They also took legal measures, which, if successful, would have meant that the custody of Mary's children remained with them.

After her release, Mary seemed happier to her family and friends. From an outside perspective, it could be easy to claim that this was just as much due to her happiness at avoiding a jail sentence as it was to her being rid of an abuser. She was in fact living with friends at first after her release, and went back to work at a dry cleaners in McMinnville, Tenn., 200 miles from Selmer.

In the same interview as was mentioned before, Mary's sisters agreed that she had changed entirely. After years of shyness, Mary seeming unable or unwilling to show love to them for fear of her husband's violence, she seemed to finally be able to open up. 'Now it's back to the old Mary [who] loves us and doesn't care to come and hug us and gives us a kiss on the cheek.'

Since then, Mary lived in McMinnville. She has moved between jobs, working at the dry cleaners, before starting work at a nursery. She briefly dated the brother of one of her most vocal supporters, Paul Pillow; afterwards, she moved in with Wayne Cantrell, a preacher living in Smithville nearby.

Mary regained custody of her three children in 2008, but by 2010, received the news that she had multiple sclerosis. Her diagnosis came at the worst time, as she was settling down in her new life; she had not long started medical school with the desire to become a nurse, and had to quit since the work would be too demanding. She hasn't returned to work since.

One comfort for Mary was that Matthew's parents seemed close to being able to forgive her. After her diagnosis, they gave Mary some time off from parenting by taking care of the children for a weekend, which soon turned into several months. Daniel Winkler has preached several times since the events on the topic of forgiveness, although when asked by local press why he chose the topic, he has refused to answer, presumably preferring to keep those details private.

Mary, too, preferred to put the past behind her. In an interview with WAFF 48, the NBC affiliate in Huntsville AL., she stated how she would prefer to stay out of the limelight, particularly for the sake of her girls. 'Whatever reason people have any problem with me, that's fine. Everybody's entitled to their opinion, but these girls are treated for who they are, not because of what their mother's done ... They're three very fine young ladies'.

Concluding Thoughts

Some members of the public reacted with disgust at the abnormally short sentence that Mary was given, and questioned whether a husband would have been given the same leniency as Mary was. Men's rights activist Glenn Sacks publicly questioned whether a man would have been shown such leniency, and pointed to the case of Scott Peterson (who received the death penalty for the murder of his pregnant wife) to indicate that no, a man would not. He also argued that the idea of abuse had been widened to include simple criticism, and should therefore not necessarily be used as defence of murder.

Conversely, there have been many women put in prison for murdering their abusive husbands, some for much longer than Mary Winkler. The 'battered woman defense', or the preferred terminology today of 'battering and its effects', is not a genuine legal defence in itself; it can, however, be used to convince a court of diminished responsibility. Its effectiveness is due to the sympathy that it elicits from jurors, who can be convinced that abuse is a form of provocation, and the murder a form of self defense. Under this defense, Mary's short sentence makes sense.

The case has remained a touch stone with regards to spousal abuse in the U.S. A made-for-TV movie, 'The Pastor's Wife', was released in 2011. It was based on the book of the same title, written by Dianne Fanning, an award winning crime writer. The story was changed somewhat, with the inclusion of a financial subplot involving tax fraud. However, it also made use of real life interviews with people who knew the Winklers- including Matthew's parents. His mother revealed that she could never believe Mary's story. Charles admitted that Mary's story could be true, and that he could forgive her if she confessed her purposeful intention to murder Matthew.

As for the community in which the family had lived, the reaction was largely one of forgiveness. According to members of that community, the town's 'Christian roots and ... its tendency to give people the benefit of the doubt' meant that they took Mary at her word. Mary's quite life in McMinnville and Smithville similarly shows that the American public would rather leave her and her family alone after their painful ordeal.

TRACEY GRISSOM

Claiming to be a victim of rape and other abuses, a distraught Tracey Grissom would travel to her ex-husband Hunter's workplace and shoot him six times in the back, receiving a twenty-five-year life sentence for his murder.

Her defense attorney would argue that Tracey was motivated by post-traumatic stress disorder caused by her Hunter's constant abuse and sexual assaults. One jury member had even asked the judge to be lenient in her sentencing as they were not allowed to hear details of her Hunter's alleged abuses (beatings, rape, sodomy).

But what really happened in the years that led up to May 15th, 2012? Was she in fact the victim of years of abuse by a psychotic husband? Or did she want to cash in on his $100,000 life insurance policy?

INSTANT ATTRACTION

The couple would meet during a dinner party in 2003 in Tuscaloosa, Alabama. Tracey was twenty-one years old and going through a divorce. She had a son, James Michael, from the previous marriage.

Family and friends would describe the union as "love at first sight." Hunter was blown away by the young Tracey's blue eyes and facial beauty.

"For him, it was love at first sight," crime author William Phelps said. "She was gorgeous."

A whirlwind courtship would ensue and the couple would elope in 2004.

"In the beginning, it was good," Tracey told CBS' 48 hours. "We had a friendship. Just your normal, honeymoon phase marriage."

"He was fun," Tracey said. "And he was attractive."

Hunter was two years younger than Tracey, however, and his mother felt that he had jumped the gun too early in the relationship.

Her words proved to be prophetic as after only eight months into the marriage, the marriage went south.

According to Tracey, their marital problems began with Hunter's drug addiction.

"I had caught him smoking marijuana," Tracey said. "Doing illegal things could cause a problem and I couldn't risk losing my son over."

Tracey claimed that she threatened her new spouse with a divorce but Hunter gave her his word that he would stop with his drug use. She stated that the relationship improved and the decided to start a construction company together.

"I took out an equity line to start a company," Tracey said. "Which was Grissom Construction. It was all in my name."

Hunter specialized in building elaborate boat docks. He had an artistic eye and could do docks, stairs, and other accouterments. The business began to grow in short order.

"They're going to take on the world," Phelps said. "They're going to be entrepreneurs and they're gonna make it."

They then had a daughter of their own, Anna Grace. The child was a long time coming for the couple. They had been trying for a long time as Tracey had five miscarriages before Anna Grace was born.

"She was premature," Tracey recalled. "Her heart and lungs were not developed. A very stressful time."

Behind closed doors things were rocky. On the surface, however, things looked good. They had a young family and were making money.

"All-American family," Phelps said. "White-picket fence. The whole nine yards. Middle-class. Suburbia. Maybe the Prince Charming that she's been waiting for."

But again, this was only on the surface. Tracey harbored secrets of her own. One of which was her own addiction to prescription drugs.

"Psychologically, there's something going on here," Phelps said. "There's something going on behind those beautiful eyes and it ain't good."

Tracey would often turn on on the children, showing off her temper. Then she would turn on Hunter.

"This would cause friction in the marriage," Phelps said. "And where there's friction, there's fire."

SETTING THE STAGE

Tracey would later state that Hunter would "act strangely" shortly before she filed divorce. She was a registered nurse and gave him an over-the-counter drug test. According to her, Hunter tested posted for marijuana, Oxycontin, opiates, and methamphetamine.

Hunter would later be arrested for marijuana possession but his family would insist that he never did the harder drugs.

Tracey would file for divorce in the summer of 2010 after six years of marriage. According to her, this would prompt physical abuse from Hunter.

Hunter had to move out but their divorce agreement would allow him access to the home.

"In September of 2010," Tracey recalled. "That was the first time he physically hit me. It (the abuse) got progressively worse. He had made the comments that if I told anybody he would kill me. I believed him."

Hunter' co-workers and family members would have a different take on the situation, however. His co-workers remembered a time when she tracked him down at one of the jobs and made a scene.

"She's screaming, jumping on him," Hunter's co-worker said. "Said something about him having another girlfriend and used the expression about, 'You are mine. I'll kill you. I'll kill you. You are mine."

"She's borderline demonic," Hunter's mother said. " mean, I absolutely believe—that she is that troubled."

Hunter's family continued to believe that he did not abuse Tracey.

"He did not have an abusive, an angry bone in his body," Hunter's aunt Gina said. "In fact, we kind of laughed at him because he was too laid-back."

The divorce was finalized in October of 2010.

EVIDENCE OF ABUSE?

Loran Richards was the first of Tracey's friends to notice the minor injuries on her body. She would inquire about the bruises but the answers she received were always evasive. Seeing Tracey with a black eye, however, forced her to try and get more answers.

"I said, Tracey, you may have terrible luck," Richards recalled. "But nobody is so unlucky that they trip, fall down the stairs, and hit their face on a baseball in the eye socket. So don't give me a lame excuse. You don't have to give me any excuse, but let's take a picture."

Tracey broke down. She gave her friend all of the grisly details, detailing the abuse she suffered at the hands of Hunter. Loran then became her advocate, taking pictures of Tracey's injuries. She would later state that she saw blood stains and other signs of abuse at Tracey's home.

THAT FATEFUL NIGHT

Now divorced, Hunter would arrive at Tracey's home on November 22nd, 2010.

According to Tracey, he then became enraged when Tracey told him that she had spent the night with a new lover.

"He told me that he was gonna kill me," Tracey recalled. Tracey stated that she tried to escape, running into the closet in order to "get away from the kids and to pray." Tracey's eleven-year-old son from a previous relationship was in the home as was the four-year-old daughter they have together.

Hunter caught up with her and knocked her to the ground. He tied a belt around her ankles and then began choking her.

Half-conscious, Tracey alleged to have been raped and sodomized.

The brutal attack would leave Tracey unconscious. She would wake up the next morning on the bathroom floor.

"I called Hunter," Tracey recalled. "I told him that I was bleeding and that I was hurt and that I needed help. And he told me, 'Fuck you. I hope you die."

Tracey wound up in the emergency room after the attack. Hospital records would show that she had a laceration on her head, bruises, and ligature marks on her feet.

Tracey would then be referred to the Turning Point domestic violence center.

Marian Waters would describe Tracey's injuries as among the worst she had ever seen in a twenty-year career.

Waters would testify that Tracey had suffered a horrific assault. She described her mental state as typical of someone who had just been raped; fearful, jumpy, fearing for her life.

Tracey had suffered a hematoma on her side that was the side of a grapefruit. She also claimed to have experienced rectal nerve damage which would require surgery as well as torn vaginal muscles requiring her to have a hysterectomy.

Police were called and Hunter would be arrested for rape, sodomy, kidnapping and domestic violence.

"And at that point, I feared for my life," Tracey recalled. "And I feared for my children's life."

A HIDDEN AGENDA

Hunter would be freed on bail but Tracey got a restraining order against him. She bought a gun and did not go anywhere unarmed.

She took photos of her injuries on the night of the alleged attack and texted them to Loran. Later, they would take more pictures.

Angered, Hunter would stop paying her spousal and child support. Tracey, however, may have had another scenario in mind for obtaining money.

She had forced Hunter to take out a $103,000 life insurance policy around the time their daughter was born.

On May 24, 2012, the day before Tracey shot Hunter, she would place a call to MetLife that was recorded.

"Thank you for calling MetLife, this is Pam. May I please have your name?"

"Tracey Grissom."

Tracey would then explain that she was angry that her husband stopped making payments on his policy. During their divorce proceedings, he had agreed to continue paying the premiums. Tracey stated she was calling to make sure that they had the correct address on file.

"Is there anything else I can do for you today?

"That's gonna be it!" Tracey said, hanging up.

"Well, May 14th was just like any other day," Tracey said, explaining the call to the insurance company. "However, I had moved four different times. Me and my children were running. We were running from Hunter. So I had called the company to let them know that they had my old address and to make an address change."

FALSE RAPE?

Shelly Standridge was hired by Hunter to defend him in the rape case. She would state that Hunter denied raping or even assaulting Tracey that night. Hunter did, however, admit to the fact that he and his wife had consensual sex that night...Rough consensual sex.

"So that night," Standridge said. "Hunter said that she was depressed and claiming she was going to kill herself. She was saying she wanted their relationship to work."

So she undressed in front of him. Her beauty was always impossible for Hunter to resist.

The two had sex despite Hunter having a new girlfriend at home.

Hunter's aunt, Gina, believed that Tracey wanted to kill Hunter before the rape case went to court.

"He had a new girlfriend, he was living with her," Phelps said. "He was moving on with his life. Hunter would claim that Tracey was jealous, obsessive, even stalked them."

"Hunter had moved on," Hunter's aunt said. "There was some court dates coming up that would prove that Hunter was innocent. There were court dates coming up that he would get visitation to his daughter. She had a lot to lose."

Tracey was on the anti-anxiety drug Klonopin. Hunter would tell his attorney that Tracey would take more than her prescribed dose. Because of this, she fell and cut her head. Hunter would then leave the house around 10:30 pm and go to his father's house. Tracey would call him hours later, at 3:20 am.

Hunter would state that Tracey had called to threaten him. She told him if he didn't want the responsibility of the children then she would make it where he would never be able to see them again.

Hunter's attorney did not know what Tracey's motive was for crying rape. She was very upset that he had a girlfriend.

MORE LIES...

Hunter would be arrested nearly twelve hours later, to his total shock.

Tracey would give her side of the story to the police which later is proven to be false.

She would tell police that Hunter had thrown her against the bathtub around 10 pm and claim to be unconscious until 4 am the next morning.

"But her phone records show she was on the phone all night, so she was never unconscious," Standridge said. "She was also using her data at 10:42 that night. She was using it again at 10:50 that night. ... She sends a text to her boyfriend at 1:49 am. She sends a text to her friend at 2:07 am. She sends another text to her boyfriend at 2:07 am."

Tracey would blame the calls on Hunter.

"All I do know is I was not the only person using my phone that night," Tracey said, suggesting that Hunter used her phone.

Medical records would show that Tracey's head wound was "purely superficial".

Only one suture was needed.

Furthermore, there was nothing on the medical record to support the fact that Tracey experienced vaginal and rectal tears. She did have bruises on her ankle and legs but the photos taken by police at the emergency room would not resemble the same photos that Tracey and her friend Loran would take days later. In the photos taken at the emergency room, an area of Tracey's body has no bruises. Days later, there is discoloration.

Tracey's attorney would blame the discrepancy on "blood thinners" which would cause Tracey to bruise easily.

There was also a discrepancy in her phone records. She would take a photo of her inner thigh, a deep bruise. This area of her body was not photographed by police during her emergency room visit. But on December 9th, almost two weeks later, Tracey took a photo of her inner thigh with the deep bruise

"He (Hunter) told me that he would make it to where nobody would ever want me," Tracey said after a 2010 attack. "I didn't report it because I thought he would kill me."

THE FINAL STRAW

Tracey woke up pissed on May 15th, 2012.

Hunter had been ordered to pay $2,100 a month for the rest of his life. He was not complying with the court order claiming that he was "out of work."

Tracey stated that she was on her way to a job interview when she saw a Grissom Construction sign out of the corner of her eye.

She stated that her initial plan was to take a photograph of Hunter at the job site in order to show proof that he was working as part of her litigation.

"I was getting ready to take the picture and when I looked up he was standing almost directly towards the front of the boat trailer," Tracey said. "He was looking back directly at me. He had this face, that's like mean - just, I don't know how to describe it. I mean, I see it over and over like it's right there all the time. He flipped me the bird, which to me was kinda like, 'Yeah I'm workin. Screw you.' And at that point, I panicked. At that point, I didn't know what else to do except to defend myself."

Tracey started firing. The first shot hit Hunter in the arm. He started to run and she fired again repeatedly. One of the bullets punctured Hunter's heart and he died of massive internal bleeding.

William Dockery was working with Hunter and was an eyewitness to the shooting. Hunter had turned to Dockery before the shooting and told him to "call the law". Before Dockery could pick up his cell phone, Tracey had commenced shooting.

Tracey then pulled out her own cell phone and called the cops on herself. She tearfully described that she had just murdered her husband.

CONFESSION

Tracey told detectives exactly what was going through her mind when she came upon Hunter at the construction site.

"Tell me about what happened," the detective said. "What led up to...what's going on."

"In November of 2010, he beat me unconscious and raped me...and, and left me for dead....and, and I finally pressed charges against him and he told me that he would make my life a living hell...and that's what he's done."

"What, what happened this morning that led up to you going..."

"I was going to work and I saw him...and he's been claiming that he-he's not working. And, so I pulled in there to take a picture of him...cause it was the truck that's still in my name...and the boat that's still in my name...and the trailer that's still in my name...He just stared at me and flipped me off...and I just went in there and shot him...I just shot him, I shot him, and I shot him."

Tracey would be distraught and tearful during her interrogation room confession. A few weeks later, however, she would call the insurance company to let them know that Hunter had died.

"Well, I was actually calling because I didn't know what I needed to do ... Hunter passed away May 15th and I actually am going a court case right now because it was due to self-defense..."

Hunter's family went ballistic over this. Tracey would claim that she had no money but she continued to pay his life insurance premiums.

"Even through the times when she's screamin' that she's destitute and has no money ... she continued to pay life insurance premium," Hunter's mother said.

"I don't think my sister concocted a story," Tracey's sister said. "Just so she could get insurance money. ... But that's all they (the prosecution) had."

THE TRIAL

Tracey's allegations of rape and sodomy would not be allowed in court testimony. She was allowed, however, to detail the effects of Hunter's abuse on her were.

Taking the stand, Tracey would lift up her shirt in court and show herself wearing a colostomy bag. She stated that she had undergone several surgeries after her husband's daily rapes wherein she suffered permanent rectal and vaginal damage.

Hunter's family was then allowed to speak at the hearing.

"This tremendous loss has changed me," Hunter's mother, Melanie Garner said. "And I don't know how to change back."

Chloe, Hunter's sister, had a victim's services officer read her letter in court.

"Tracey is psychotic," Chloe wrote. "She is the most selfish person human being on this earth."

"Every mother should pray every night that your son doesn't fall in love with someone like Tracey," Hunter's aunt, Gina Grissom said. "There have been lots of allegations against Hunter. We've never believed anything that has come out of her (Tracey's) mouth."

His aunt then looked directly at Tracey.

"Hunter was proud of his name. Why would you still choose to use our name, and bring it down?" suggesting that if Tracey hated him so much why didn't she go revert to her maiden name after the divorce.

The jurors would find Tracey guilty of murder. She would be sentenced to twenty-five years in prison.

One of the jurors, Janice Kelly, would contact Grissom's attorney Warren Freeman the morning after the trial. She had remorse over her decision and said that she wouldn't have convicted her had they had the rapes and abuse allegations been introduced as evidence.

"I feel I made a mistake," Kelly said. "If I had to do it over again, we'd have had a hung jury. We didn't get her side. She did not get a fair trial."

"We voted to convict because there was no dispute that Tracey shot Hunter," the jury foreman wrote in a letter that was addressed in the courthouse. "Jurors didn't believe prosecutor claims that she did it in order to collect a life insurance policy. We felt the shooting was a crime of passion, not for financial gain and that she should be sentenced accordingly. I wish we had seen evidence of the rape allegation. We feel that she just 'lost it.'"

"It's not fair, it's not fair!" Tracey sobbed as she was led out of the courthouse and to jail.

"We think the sentencing was too harsh," Tracey's attorney Warren Freeman said. "Considering you have the foreperson of the jury actually saying, we don't feel like she should be punished according to being found guilty of murder. Let's just say that there will be a basis for a new trial, and part of it will be something that the jurors saw that they weren't supposed to see and I'm going to just leave it at that until I file my motion."

"My son died running for his life," Hunter's mother said. "I don't know what was running through his mind but I hear him say 'momma.'"

"People who think that I murdered him in cold blood," Tracey said. "Either don't know the whole story or don't know everything that's happened.

Tracey was asked on CBS' 48 hours if she regretted pulling the trigger on that fateful day.

"No," she said flatly. "Because if I hadn't I would be dead. I truly believe that."

"She has a way of making everything she does look right," Hunter's aunt, Gina scoffed.

TED BUNDY

Ted Bundy is one of the most prolific serial killers of the 20th century, having kidnapped, raped, and murdered at least 36 attractive young women between 1973 and 1978 in Colorado, Oregon, Utah, Florida, and Washington; however, many assert that this figure could be much higher. He had also kept some of his victims' body parts—including heads—as trophies in a utility shed behind his Utah home, as well having engaged in necrophilia with decomposing corpses which he would groom and apply makeup.

A master manipulator and classic antisocial personality, Bundy escaped custody twice; once from court during his first murder trial and the second time from the Garfield County Jail in Colorado by sawing a hole in his cell ceiling. He was placed on the FBI's Ten Most Wanted list and was later arrested in Florida in February 1978 after stealing a car. He was sentenced to death in 1979 for the murder of two Florida State University sorority sisters, and again in 1980 for another murder.

Very charismatic and handsome, Bundy exploited these characteristics heavily with his young female victims in an effort to earn their sympathy trust. He would often approach potential victims in public places, feigning injury or impersonating an authority figure before overpowering them—usually by hitting them in the head with a crowbar—taking them to secluded locations, and raping and murdering them. Sometimes he would simply break into young women's homes and bludgeon them while they slept.

Bundy was originally incarcerated for aggravated kidnapping and attempted assault in 1975 in Utah; however, his list of homicide victims continued to grow. He escaped from custody twice in Colorado and subsequently committed three more murders before finally being apprehended in Florida in 1978. Ted Bundy was sentenced to death and was executed in the electric chair at Raiford Prison in Starke, Florida, on 24 January 1989.

Early Life

Theodore Robert Bundy—originally Theodore Robert Cowell—was born on 24 November 1946 at the Elizabeth Lund Home for Unwed Mothers in Burlington, Vermont. The social stigma of being a single mother was great at that time so Bundy's mother, Louise Cowell, took her infant son to live with her parents—Samuel and Eleanor—in Philadelphia where young Ted took on the Cowell surname and was told that they were, in fact, his parents and that his mother was his sister. Eventually, Bundy discovered the truth and harbored lifelong resentment toward his mother for lying to him.

Bundy's paternity has never been definitively proven. His birth certificate lists his father as Lloyd Marshall, an Air Force veteran and salesman; however, Louise has claimed that she was "seduced by 'a sailor'" whose name "may have been Jack Worthington" but nobody by that name was ever found in Navy or merchant marines records. Compounding the problem is that Bundy's grandfather, Samuel Cowell, has been rumored to be his biological father; thus making Bundy the product of incest; however, again, there is no evidence of this.

In interviews, Bundy spoke highly of his grandparents, especially expressing a fondness for his grandfather even though other family members described Samuel as a tyrannical bully and bigot who beat his wife and dog, abused his daughters, harmed neighborhood cats, and would sometimes "speak aloud to unseen presences". Bundy's grandmother was timid and obedient and was treated for her depression with electroconvulsive therapy.

Bundy exhibited disturbing behavior from a young age. At the age of three, he was alleged to have surrounded his sleeping aunt, Julia, with household knives—blades pointed toward her—and smiled at her when she had awakened.

In 1950, when Bundy was only four, Louise changed both her and her son's surname to Nelson and moved them both to Tacoma, Washington, to live with cousins Jane and Alan Scott. In 1951, Louise met hospital cook Johnny Culpepper Bundy at a church singles night and they married later that year. Johnny formally adopted young Ted and he adopted the last name of Bundy. Even with efforts to include young Ted in family activities along with his four half-siblings—who he was often left to babysit—he always was distant. Later, Bundy would tell his girlfriend that Johnny wasn't his real dad, wasn't smart enough, and didn't make much money.

Bundy confessed that he "chose to be alone" as an adolescent and neither had any natural inclination to develop any close friendships nor knew what drove people to be friends in the first place. He would later say that he "hit a wall" and his inability to comprehend social behavior stunted his social development, rendering him required to adopt a façade of social activity. He was terribly shy, self-doubting, and uncomfortable in social situations and often teased for being different. Despite this, he was a good student at Woodrow Wilson High School, was active in a local Methodist church, and was even involved with a local Boy Scout troop.

Bundy would also admit—while on death row—that a part of him as a young child was "fascinated by images of sex and violence" and he called this part "the entity". He enjoyed reading crime books and detective magazines, particularly those that contained descriptions of sexual violence and pictures of dead bodies. Later, before his execution, he would admit that pornography was central in shaping who he was.

Throughout high school Bundy loved to ski and was very good at it; however, his pursuit of this hobby was usually accomplished with stolen equipment and forged lift tickets. He was also arrested on at least two occasions on suspicion of auto theft and burglary but when he turned 18 his juvenile record was expunged. Stealing, for Bundy, did not involve any guilt and, in fact, he had a sense of entitlement about the entire thing. He often said that the thrill of taking possession of something he wanted without remorse was exciting. Many speculate that his "taking" of his victims represented this same concept and provided him with the same rush. Compounding the problem was his sense of entitlement and cunning ability to lie about everything which demonstrates a common trait among psychopaths.

Bundy graduated high school in 1965 and was awarded a scholarship by the University of Puget Sound where he started that fall, taking courses in Oriental studies and psychology. After two semesters he transferred to the University of Washington in Seattle.

He obtained employment as a stock boy and bagger at a Safeway store on Queen Anne Hill, in addition to other odd jobs. As part of his psychology curricula, he would work as a night-shift volunteer at Seattle's Suicide Hot Line where he met and worked Ann Rule who would later become among the world's foremost true crime writers and who penned a biography about Bundy—that was also partly autobiographical about her working relationship with him—entitled *The Stranger Beside Me* (1980).

While in college, circa 1968, Bundy began a relationship with fellow student "Stephanie Brooks" (a pseudonym); however, after she graduated in 1968 and prepared to move back home to California she broke up with Bundy due to what she described as his lack of ambition and immaturity. Bundy was heartbroken after this and, interestingly, all of his victims bore some resemblance to Brooks; particularly the fact that Brooks and all of his victims had long dark hair which they wore parted down the middle.

Shortly thereafter, Bundy returned to Burlington—his birthplace—and learned the truth of his parentage. This discovery made him more dominant and focused.

He managed the Seattle office of Nelson Rockefeller's presidential campaign in 1968 and attended the 1968 Republican convention in Miami, Florida. He reenrolled at the University of Washington with a major in psychology. He became popular among his professors as he was an honor student and also began a relationship with Elizabeth Kloepfer in 1969. Kloepfer was a divorced secretary with a young daughter and the two dated for the next six years until he went to prison in 1976.

Bundy graduated in 1972 with a degree in psychology and went to work for the state Republican Party.

In the fall of 1973, Bundy enrolled in the University of Utah Law School but did poorly because of poor attendance and, consequently, dropped out the following spring.

While in California on a business trip in the summer of 1973, Bundy found his ex-girlfriend "Stephanie Brooks" and the change in his look and attitude was appealing to her. Bundy courted Brooks the rest of the year—while still involved with Kloepfer—and proposed to her, only to dump Brooks shortly after the new year, likely in retaliation for her breaking his heart years earlier. The breakup wreaked havoc on Bundy who became obsessed with her and this obsession "would span his lifetime and lead to a series of events that would shock the world".

Mere weeks later, Bundy began his first murderous rampage in Washington; however, many Bundy experts assert that he likely starting killing in his teens. One case involved eight-year-old Ann Marie Burr from Tacoma who disappeared from her home in 1961 when Bundy was 14. Burr's house was on Bundy's newspaper delivery route and her father was positive that he saw Bundy near a construction site ditch on the nearby University of Puget Sound campus the day his daughter vanished. Despite other potentially incriminating circumstantial evidence, Bundy remains merely a suspect due to a lack of consensus by law enforcement personnel as to whether they believe he actually did it or not. Bundy has always denied killing her.

Shortly before his execution, Bundy did, in fact, tell his attorney that his first attempt at kidnapping was in 1969 and his first "actual murder" occurred "sometime in 1972". While he was a suspect in the December 1973 murder of Kathy Devine in Washington, DNA analysis exonerated him and her true murderer was convicted in 2002.

Bundy's earliest identified murders were committed in 1974 when he was 27.

Bundy was a handsome and charismatic guy, particularly to his young female victims and he exploited these characteristics fully. He was also an adept chameleon, able to blend in and feign belonging which increased his threat to the attractive brunette women he targeted as his victims. This charm and his adroitness at lying and manipulation made him extremely dangerous.

Known Murder Victims

Karen Sparks (often referred to as Joni Lenz), 18 (survived)

On 4 January 1974, 18-year-old Karen Sparks/Joni Lenz was found by her roommates when she didn't emerge from her bedroom that morning. They were not prepared for what horrific sights they saw. Sparks had been beaten badly and a bed rod ripped from the bed was "savagely rammed into her vagina". Sparks was transported to the hospital in a coma and suffered damages which continue to plague her.

However, she was one of the lucky few victims to survive an attack by Bundy.

Lynda Ann Healy, 21

A very accomplished and beautiful young woman, 21-year-old Lynda Healy announced ski conditions for all of the western Washington resorts on the radio. A senior at the University of Washington, she came from a good family, loved to sing, and was majoring in psychology. She shared a house with four other young women near the university. On 31 January, Healy and some friends went to a tavern and then home to bed. Her roommate in the next room never heard any sounds emanating from Healy's room that night.

The following morning when she didn't emerge from her bedroom after her alarm clock sounded at its usual 5:30 a.m. to go to work—and her job called looking for her—her roommate noticed that her bed was made in a peculiar way. Further inspection showed that the top sheet and a pillowcase were missing, a small bloodstain that was the same type as Lynda's was on the pillow and the bottom sheet, and a bloody nightgown was hanging in her closet. One of her outfits was missing. Also worrisome was that one of the doors was unlocked.

Initially, due to the absence of fingerprint, hair, or fiber evidence, police did not suspect foul play; however, later, they did come to realize that an intruder came in, removed Healy's nightgown and dressed her in another outfit, made the bed, wrapped her up, and took her out of the house.

Donna Gail Manson, 19

On 12 March, in Olympia, 19-year-old Evergreen State College student Donna Manson was kidnapped and murdered.

Susan Elaine Rancourt, 18

On 17 April, Susan Rancourt, 18, disappeared from the Central Washington State College campus in Ellensburg while walking across campus, alone, at night.

Later, two other female coeds would report meeting a good-looking man with his arm in a cast—one the night Rancourt disappeared and one three nights earlier—who asked for assistance with carrying books to his VW Beetle.

Roberta Kathleen "Kathy" Parks, 22

Kathy Parks, 22, was last seen on 6 May on the Oregon State University campus in Corvallis en route to meeting friends for coffee.

Brenda Carol Ball, 22

22-year-old Brenda Ball was last seen leaving the Flame Tavern in Burien, Oregon on 1 June.

Georgeann Hawkins, 18

In the early morning hours of 11 June, University of Washington student and a member of Kappa Alpha Theta Georgeann Hawkins, 18, left her boyfriend's dormitory en route to her sorority house through an alley. She was never seen again; however, witnesses later stated they had seen a man with a leg cast struggling to carry a briefcase in that area. Another female coed reported that he had asked her for help in carrying his briefcase to his VW Beetle.

Bundy later confessed to having lured Hawkins to his car, clubbed her with a tire iron he had hidden underneath his vehicle, and then took her elsewhere to rape and strangle her to death.

Janice Ann Ott, 23, and Denise Marie Naslund, 19

On 14 July, Janet Ott, 23, and Denise Naslund, 19, were abducted mere hours apart from Lake Sammamish State Park in Issaquah, Washington, in broad daylight. On that day, eight different witnesses reported seeing a handsome young man with his arm in a sling who called himself "Ted" and who asked several women for help unloading a sailboat from his VW Beetle. One witness said she walked with him for a ways but didn't see a sailboat and then declined to help him. Other witnesses stated that they saw the man approach Ott and she was observed walking away with him.

Naslund disappeared four hours later.

At this point, police in King County put up fliers with the suspected murderer's description all over the Seattle area. One of Bundy's psychology professors, former coworker Ann Rule, and Bundy's girlfriend Elizabeth Kloepfer reported him as a possible suspect. In fact, Kloepfer (who since changed her surname to Kendall and penned a book called *The Phantom Prince: My Life with Ted Bundy* in 1981) told the Seattle Police Department that her boyfriend "might be involved" in the recent Seattle murders. She called again later that autumn with more information and agreed to give them recent pictures of Bundy to be shown to witnesses; however, many of them could not positively identify him.

Ott's and Naslund's remains were found on 7 September off Interstate 90 near Issaquah, only one mile from the park where they were abducted. Near the women's remains was an extra femur and vertebrae which Bundy confessed before his execution belonged to Hawkins.

Between 1 March and 3 March 1975, the skulls and jawbones belonging to Healy, Rancourt, Parks, and Ball were found just east of Issaquah on Taylor Mountain. Bundy confessed in his death row interview that he kept the decapitated heads of these four victims in his apartment for some time and that he would revisit this dump site often to engage in sex with the corpses until decomposition became too great to continue. Bundy also admitted that he dumped Manson's body there as well—but burned her skull in his girlfriend's fireplace—however, no trace of her was ever recovered.

Other trophies discovered when Bundy's apartment was searched include photographs of his victims and a large bag of women's clothing.

Nancy Wilcox, 16

Bundy began the University of Utah Law School in the autumn of 1974. On 2 October 1974, 16-year-old Nancy Wilcox disappeared from Holladay, Utah. She was last seen in a VW Beetle.

Melissa Smith, 17

On 18 October, 17-year-old Melissa Smith—the daughter of Midvale, Utah's Police Chief Louis Smith—disappeared after leaving a pizza parlor. Nine days later she was found strangled, raped, and sodomized.

Laura Aime, 17

17-year-old Laura Aime disappeared from a Halloween party in Lehi, Utah. Her naked corpse was found on Thanksgiving Day by hikers near a river in the Wasatch Mountains. She had been beaten about the head and face with a crowbar and was raped and sodomized. The lack of blood at the crime scene indicated that she was likely killed elsewhere and dumped in this location. Police found no other physical evidence.

Carol DaRonch, 18 (survived)

On 8 November, 18-year-old Carol DaRonch was shopping at the Fashion Place Mall in Salt Lake City, Utah, and was approached by a man in the Sears parking lot who claimed to be a police officer named Officer Roseland. He told her that her car had been stolen and that he would take her to the police station to retrieve it. He took her to his VW Beetle and she became suspicious and asked him for identification. He quickly flashed a gold badge and she got in but refused his order to fasten her seat belt. After a short distance, Bundy pulled over and attempted to place handcuffs on DaRonch but only managed one wrist. He also attempted to hit her with a crowbar which she was able to catch before it hit her head. DaRonch fought back, kicking him in the groin, and as the car was speeding away she jumped out of it.

DaRonch flagged down another car and they took her to the police who confirmed there was no Officer Roseland. Police were able to obtain a description of the assailant and his car and a blood sample from DaRonch's coat. Type O; the same as Bundy's.

Debra Kent, 17

Mere hours after losing DaRonch Bundy abducted 17-year-old Debra "Debi" Kent from the parking lot of a school in Bountiful, Utah, as she was leaving a school play. She had told her parents she was going to pick up her brother at the bowling alley and she would be back to pick them up soon but never returned. She didn't even make it to her car which was still in the parking lot. Police found a small handcuff key in the parking lot and when they tried the key in the handcuffs DaRonch was wearing, it was a perfect fit.

A month later a man called the police and told them that he saw a tan VW Beetle speeding away from the high school parking lot the night Kent disappeared.

Shortly before he was to be executed, Bundy confessed that he dumped Kent's body near Fairview, Utah. After an intense search of the area, a human kneecap which was consistent with someone of Kent's age and size was found; however, DNA analysis was not conducted.

Caryn Campbell, 23

Bundy's first murder of 1975 occurred on 12 January. 23-year-old Michigan nurse Caryn Campbell disappeared between her hotel's lounge and her room while on a ski trip with her fiancé, Dr. Raymond Gadowski, and his two children, in Snowmass, Colorado. Frantic Gadowski called the police the next morning but a search proved futile.

Nearly a month later—and only a few short miles from where she went missing—a recreational worker discovered Campbell's nude body near the road. Animal damage to her body made it difficult to determine the exact cause of death; however, there was evidence of repeated, crushing blows to her head by a sharp instrument. Some of the blows were so violent that one of her teeth separated from the gums.

Julie Cunningham, 26

On 15 March, 26-year-old Vail ski instructor Julie Cunningham disappeared on her way to a nearby tavern. Bundy confessed in prison that he used his crutches ploy to approach Cunningham to ask for her help carrying ski boots to his car before he clubbed her with his crowbar, handcuffed her, and took her to a secluded location where strangled her.

Denise Oliverson, 25

25-year-old Denise Oliverson vanished in Grand Junction on 6 April while riding her bicycle to visit her parents.

Lynette Culver, 13

13-year-old Lynette Culver was abducted from her school playground at Alameda Junior High School in Pocatello, Idaho.

Susan Curtis, 15

Once Bundy returned to Utah, 15-year-old Susan Curtis vanished on 28 June while walking alone to the Brigham Young University dormitories during a youth conference she was attending. Bundy confessed to her murder minutes before his execution.

The bodies of Cunningham, Oliverson, Culver, and Curtis have never been found.

First Arrest, Trial, and Escapes

Bundy was first arrested on 16 August 1975 in Salt Lake City for failure to stop his vehicle for police. A search of his car unearthed a crowbar, handcuffs, ski mask, trash bags, an icepick, and other items the officer thought were burglary tools. The always calm and collected Bundy explained reasons why he had the items such as that he used the mask for skiing and had found the handcuffs in a dumpster; however, Detective Jerry Thompson connected Bundy and his Volkswagen to the DaRonch kidnapping and other missing girls and searched his apartment.

The search yielded a brochure of Colorado ski resorts with a checkmark by where Campbell had disappeared. Bundy was brought in for a lineup before DaRonch and other witnesses at the time DaRonch was kidnapped and they all identified him as Officer Roseland, as well as the man lurking about on the night Debbie Kent vanished.

After a week-long trial, Bundy was convicted on 1 March 1976 of kidnapping DaRonch and was sentenced to 15 years in Utah State Prison. Bundy was then extradited to Colorado to stand trial for murder.

He was able to escape custody twice before his eventual final arrest in Florida. The first escape occurred on 7 June 1977, when he was transported from the Garfield County Jail in Glenwood Springs, Colorado, to Pitkin County Courthouse in Aspen for his preliminary hearing. As he was serving as his own attorney, the judge excused him from being handcuffed and shackled. During a recess Bundy asked if he could research his case in the courthouse's law library. Hiding behind a bookcase he jumped from a second-story window, spraining his ankle when he landed. After shedding his suit, he simply walked through the town of Aspen as roadblocks were being erected before hiking southward on Aspen Mountain.

Near its summit he burglarized a cabin and stole clothing, food, and a rifle before heading toward Crested Butte; however, Bundy became lost and ended up wandering aimlessly for two days before breaking into a camping trailer on Maroon Lake where he took more food and a parka. Bundy then walked back toward Aspen and stole a car parked at the Aspen Golf Course. Two police officers noticed him weaving in traffic and pulled over the six-day fugitive. In the car were maps of the mountains around Aspen that the prosecutor was using to demonstrate where victim Caryn Campbell's body was found. As Bundy was his own attorney, he had the right of discovery to this evidence, thus demonstrating that he had planned his escape.

Bundy's second escape occurred on 30 December 1977, after having his motion for a change of venue to Denver accepted but with the venue being Colorado Springs instead; a city that had historically been hostile to murder suspects. He had managed to acquire the jail's floor plan and a hacksaw blade from other inmates, as well as $500 in cash smuggled in over a six-month period by visitors—particularly one Carole Ann Boone. In the evening while other inmates were showering, Bundy sawed a one-foot-square hole in his cell's ceiling—behind the steel bars—and was able to fit through it into the crawlspace above after losing 35 pounds. Prior to his actual escape, Bundy "practiced" and multiple reports of possible movement in the ceiling's crawlspace were, curiously, never investigated.

On the night of his escape, Bundy piled files and books under his covers in his bunk to look like his sleeping body, climbed into the crawlspace, broke through the jail's ceiling which, incidentally, was the chief jailer's apartment who just happened to be out for the evening with his wife. Bundy stole some street clothes and casually sauntered out the front door.

Bundy stole a car and drove east; however, the car broke down on Colorado's Interstate 70. A passing motorist gave him a ride into Vail where he caught a bus to Denver and then took a flight to Chicago, Illinois. From there he took an Amtrak train to Ann Arbor, Michigan.

His escape was discovered over 17 hours after the fact at noon on New Year's Eve.

Lisa Levy, 20, Margaret Bowman, 21, Karen Chandler (survived), Kathy Kleiner Deshields (survived)

On 15 January 1978—after Bundy had escaped from jail in Colorado, he traveled to Tallahassee, Florida, and attacked Chi Omega sorority sisters at Florida State University. At approximately 3:00 a.m. he entered the sorority house where he raped and strangled 20-year-old Lisa Levy to death; bludgeoned 21-year-old Margaret Bowman to death; and also bludgeoned Karen Chandler and Kathy Kleiner—both of whom survived.

The entire rampage took only 30 minutes.

Cheryl Thomas (survived)

That same morning, a mere eight blocks from the Chi Omega sorority house, Bundy attacked Cheryl Thomas in her bed and bludgeoned her with a wooden club, severely injuring her.

Kimberly Leach, 12

On 9 February, Bundy kidnapped 12-year-old Kimberly Leach from her junior high school in Lake City, Florida. Her raped, murdered, and dumped body was found in Suwannee River State Park underneath a small pig shed.

Bundy then stole another VW Beetle and left Tallahassee, traveling west across the Florida panhandle.

Florida Arrest

On 15 February 1978 shortly after 1:00 a.m., Bundy was stopped by Pensacola police officer David Lee who learned that the vehicle was stolen. After a brief scuffle, Lee had subdued and restrained Bundy and then took him to jail. During the transport, Bundy allegedly told Lee that he wished the officer would have killed him. Once his identity was confirmed, Bundy was transported to Tallahassee and charged with the Tallahassee and Lake City murders.

Florida Trials and Convictions

Among the most damning evidence during Bundy's June 1979 Chi Omega murder trial were bite marks found on Lisa Levy's left buttock which matched a plaster cast taken from Bundy's mouth. Additionally, Chi Omega sister Nita Neary was returning home late that night and saw Bundy as he left. She was able to identify him in court.

Bundy was convicted on all counts and sentenced to death.

In 1980, Bundy stood trial for the Kimberly Leach murder. Again, he was convicted, this time based upon fiber evidence and an eyewitness who saw him leading Leach away from the school. Bundy was, again, sentenced to death.

After his sentences he sought a stay of execution or commutation of his death sentences to life imprisonment by having one of his legal advocates contact his victims' families to ask them to ask for mercy in order to find out where their loved ones' remains were. This ploy for more time failed.

Execution

Bundy ultimately met his demise in Raiford Prison's electric chair on 24 January 1989.

Shortly before his widely-publicized execution, Bundy confessed to 36 murders in seven states; however, many believe that the total number is much higher. Also before his execution, Bundy contacted Dr. James Dobson, psychologist and founder of the Christian evangelical organization Focus on the Family, and agreed to a television interview the day before his execution. In it, Bundy described the influence of pornography on his behavior. While not expressly blaming pornography for his behavior, Bundy did say that pornographic materials shaped and molded his behavior and he would gradually need more violent, graphic, and explicit material to achieve the same "high"; not unlike a drug addict. He claimed that while murdering he was "possessed by 'something ... awful and alien'" and the brutal urge was indescribable. He also claimed that alcohol helped remove the initial boundary for him to commit his first murder. Bundy also admitted that although he believed he deserved the death penalty, he didn't want to die.

Even today, Bundy remains a suspect in a number of open homicide cases and is likely responsible for other victims who will never be identified. In 1987 he confided to Keppel that there were some murders that he would "never talk about" because they were committed too close to home, involved victims who were very young, or were too close to family. Said victims include the aforementioned Ann Marie Burr who Bundy repeatedly denied having murdered; however, Keppel noticed that Burr fits all three of Bundy's "no discussion" categories. In 2011, forensic testing of material from the Burr crime scene did not have enough intact DNA sequences to compare to Bundy's.

Additional potential victims include flight attendants Lisa E. Wick and Lonnie Trumbull, both 20, who were bludgeoned with a piece of wood while asleep in their Seattle home on 23 June 1966 that was very near the Safeway store where Bundy worked at the time, and where the victims regularly shopped. Trumbull did not make it and Wick suffered permanent memory loss.

On 30 May 1969 college friends Susan Davis and Elizabeth Perry, both 19, who were on vacation in Atlantic City, New Jersey—just 60 miles south of Philadelphia—were found stabbed to death in the woods three days later.

On 19 July 1971, 24-year-old elementary school teacher and motel maid Rita Curran was murdered in her basement apartment in Burlington, Vermont. She had been bludgeoned, raped, and strangled. The motel where she worked part-time was adjacent to the Elizabeth Lund Home where Bundy was born and certain similarities to his other crime scenes made Bundy a suspect.

21-year-old Joyce LePage was last seen alive on 22 July 1971 on the Washington State University campus. Nine months later her skeleton was found wrapped in military blankets, carpeting, and rope, at the bottom of a Pullman, Washington, ravine.

On 29 June 1973, 17-year-old Rita Lorraine Jolly disappeared from West Linn, Oregon while 24-year-old Vicki Lynn Hollar disappeared from Eugene, Oregon, on 20 August of that same year. Bundy had confessed to two Oregon homicides but did not identify the victims.

Brenda Joy Baker, 14, was last seen hitchhiking near Puyallup, Washington on 27 May 1974 and her body would be discovered a month later in Millersylvania State Park.

19-year-old Wisconsin native Sandra Jean Weaver who had been living in Tooele, Utah, was last seen on 1 July 1974 in Salt Lake City. Her nude body was found the following day in Grand Junction, Colorado.

20-year-old Carol Valenzuela was last seen hitchhiking near Vancouver, Washington, on 2 August 1974 and her remains were found two months later in a shallow grave south of Olympia; along with the remains of another female who was later identified as 17-year-old Martha Morrison who was last seen in Eugene, Oregon, on 1 September 1974. During this time, Bundy drove from Seattle to Salt Lake City and could have conceivably passed through both towns; however, there is no definitive evidence.

Bundy is also a suspect in Melanie Suzanne Cooley's disappearance on 15 April 1975 after leaving Nederland High School in Nederland, Colorado. Her beaten and strangled corpse was discovered on 2 May by road maintenance workers nearby in Coal Creek Canyon. Whereas gas receipts place Bundy in Golden that day—not far from Nederland—the Jefferson County Sheriff's Office has classified her murder as a cold case.

On 1 July 1975, Shelly Kay Robertson, 24, failed to show up for work in Golden, Colorado, and her nude, decomposed corpse was found in August inside of a mine on Berthoud Pass near Winter Park. While gas station receipts place Bundy in the area, there is no direct evidence as to his complicity.

23-year-old Nancy Perry Baird disappeared from the Farmington, Utah, service station where she worked on 4 July 1975. She officially remains a missing person and Bundy has repeatedly denied involvement.

Finally, 17-year-old Debbie Smith was last seen in February 1976 in Salt Lake City before the DaRonch trial. Her body was found near the airport on 1 April 1976.

Aftermath

During the Kimberly Leach trial, Bundy married Carole Ann Boone. He took advantage of an existing Florida statute in which a marriage declaration in court in front of a judge constituted a legal marriage. Thus, Bundy called Boone as a character witness and married her while she was on the witness stand. After numerous conjugal visits, Boone gave birth to a daughter in October 1982. She returned to Washington in 1986 with her daughter after divorcing him and never returned.

Ann Rule described Bundy as "... a sadistic sociopath who took pleasure from another human's pain and the control he had over his victims, to the point of death, and even after." He once referred to himself as "the most cold-hearted son of a bitch you'll ever meet" and one of his defense attorneys, Polly Nelson, said that Bundy "was the very definition of heartless evil." At one point, Bundy said, "We serial killers are your sons, we are your husbands, we are everywhere. And there will be more of your children dead tomorrow."

Bundy contacted Robert Keppel—the detective who helped put him in prison—while on death row to assist him with the "Green River Killer" investigation at the time. With Bundy's assistance, Keppel was able to understand the inner workings of the mind of a serial killer and was, subsequently, able to identify and apprehend Gary Ridgway in November 2001.

Ted Bundy has been the subject of three television movies and one feature film. The two-part film entitled *The Deliberate Stranger* aired on NBC in 1986, starring Mark Harmon as Bundy. *Ted Bundy* (2002) starred Michael Reilly Burke as Bundy and was directed by Matthew Bright. In 2003 the USA Network aired Ann Rule's *The Stranger Beside Me* that starred Billy Campbell as Bundy and Barbara Hershey as Rule. Finally, the A&E network produced an adaptation of detective Robert Keppel's book *The Riverman* in 2004, starring Cary Elwes as Bundy and Bruce Greenwood as Keppel.

THE TRAILSIDE KILLER

David Carpenter ("Trailside Killer")

David Carpenter, also known as the Trailside Killer, stalked, sexually assaulted, and murdered mostly women on hiking trails near San Francisco, California, with a few victims in Santa Cruz, California. Most of his victims were shot in the head, execution-style, while a couple of them were stabbed to death. Carpenter's reign of terror lasted from 1979 into 1981 when he was subsequently arrested, tried, and convicted of death.

One of his victims, Stephen Haertle, survived being shot multiple times by Carpenter—even though his girlfriend Ellen Hansen was killed—and was able to give police a description of his assailant. Additional witness testimony placed a small red foreign car in the area. Carpenter matched the composite drawn from Haertle's description and he also owned a car that matched the description of the one on the scene at the time of Hansen's and Haertle's attack.

Carpenter was convicted in two separate trials; one in Los Angeles and one in San Diego. Both trials were relocated due to defense attorneys' requests for changes of venue.

He was ultimately sentenced to death and is currently on San Quentin's death row. Carpenter is 85 years of age.

Early Life

David Joseph Carpenter was born on 6 May 1930 in San Francisco—a place that would later become his hunting grounds. As a child, he was physically abused and neglected by his alcoholic father while his near-blind mother was overly domineering. By the time he was seven years old, his stutter was so bad that he couldn't function in any social situation. Many experts assert that his stuttering was likely a result of stress, self-perceived inadequacy, and not feeling safe as a child. Consequently he was ridiculed which made him overly reclusive. Instead of therapy he was forced to take ballet and piano lessons.

To relieve his frustrations, Carpenter suffered from a bedwetting problem and also tortured animals; thus fulfilling two of the three prongs of the classic serial killer triad, with the other being a preoccupation with setting fires.

From a young age he also had an insatiable sex drive and would look for opportunities to express this. At the age of 17 Carpenter was incarcerated for molesting two of his young cousins. He served a year in the custody of the California Youth Authority and apparently learned nothing because after his release he was even more predatory; offending until he got married in 1955.

Carpenter worked a number of jobs, including as a cruise ship's purser, a salesman, and a printer.

Carpenter and his wife had three children and Carpenter's demanding libido got to be too much for her. Eventually his wife was not enough to satisfy him. In addition to his violent rages he would prowl around, looking for other women. When his drive became so desperate, he resorted to violence.

By serial killer standards, Carpenter was a late bloomer. His first serious violent offense occurred in 1960 when he was arrested and incarcerated for attempted murder for attacking a woman with a hammer and knife. He had befriended this woman and invited her over to meet his wife and family. One day he picked her up for work but instead of driving her there he drove to a wooded area near the Presidio and then pretended to be lost. At some point he grabbed her, straddled her, and tied her up with a clothesline. He then threatened her with a knife, forcing her to be still and telling her that he had a "funny quirk" that needed to be satisfied. When she resisted he struck her multiple times with a hammer. Her cries for help alerted a nearby military patrol officer who, essentially, saved her life. When commanded to stop, Carpenter shot at the officer and was met with return gunfire which wounded Carpenter. He was then arrested. The victim survived. The victim described his speech to investigators as slow and deliberate, thus suggesting that when Carpenter feels as though he is in charge of a situation and asserting himself then he loses his stutter.

While initially sentenced to 14 years, Carpenter served just nine before being released in 1969. Tired of his sexual demands and temper—and having just given birth to their third child—his wife divorced him. When questioned about what caused the divorce Carpenter's story would change, thus indicating that he learned to tell people what he thought they wanted to hear.

Carpenter was remarried quickly after his release and in less than a year this marriage failed as he was back to his old tricks. He once tried to rape a woman by hitting her car to force her out of it. As she struggled with him he stabbed her but she managed to get back into her car and get help.

At this point there is little doubt that Carpenter wanted to rape again but not return to prison so he was prepared to eliminate any witnesses.

He was rearrested on 3 February 1970, in Modesto, California, on kidnapping and robbery charges. Before being transferred to prison, however, he and four other inmates escaped from the Calaveras County Jail. After recapture by the Federal Bureau of Investigation, Carpenter was incarcerated for seven years on the kidnapping and robbery charges, with two more for violating parole. He served his time and was then paroled in May 1979, without being listed as a sex offender which he should have been. In August of that year he murdered his first of many victims.

Carpenter found a job at a photo print shop in San Francisco after he left prison and by all measures appeared to be on the right path to becoming a productive and law-abiding citizen.

The Crimes

Edda Kane

44-year-old married bank executive Edda Kane disappeared from Mount Tamalpais Park near San Francisco Bay on 19 August 1979, while hiking in the part of the park nicknamed "the Sleeping Lady" to revel in the glorious view of the Golden Gate Bridge. As she enjoyed an athletic lifestyle and could not find someone to accompany her on her hike that day, she decided to go out alone. When she did not return home that day her husband called the police who sent out a search team with dogs in case she had fallen and required assistance.

Kane's vehicle was in the parking lot where she left it but there were no signs of the missing woman.

She was later found off Rock Spring Trail on 20 August 1979, naked and shot to death. Forensic experts surmised that she had been attacked from behind and then shot execution-style with a bullet in the back of the head based upon the position of her body on its knees with her face in the dirt. $10 was missing from her wallet, along with some credit cards. The attacker took her glasses but left her jewelry.

This was the first murder on Mount Tamalpais.

Kane's autopsy demonstrated that she had been shot once in the back of the head with a .44 caliber gun. As she had not been raped, police were dumbfounded as to the motive for the attack. Nobody who knew the victim could think of anyone who would want to do her any harm and the lack of evidence did not permit police to fully investigate her death. After a short time her murder became an unsolved isolated homicide and things returned to normal until the following spring.

Barbara Schwartz

On 7 March 1980, 23-year-old baker Barbara Schwartz had gone hiking in Mount Tamalpais State Park with her dog and had never returned.

She was found on a narrow unpaved trail, stabbed to death in the chest. A witness who had watched the entire crime ran for help and, thus, led the rangers to the crime scene. The witness was hiking in the area when she saw through the trees a thin, athletic man, about 25 years of age approach Schwartz whose dog was barking. She said the assailant "had a hawk nose and dark hair, and he wore hiking boots." The witness then stated that the man and victim struggled for nearly a minute and then he left as Schwartz fell to the ground which was when she left to seek help. Unfortunately, the witness' description of the assailant was "wildly erroneous in every respect" and she, in fact, later admitted this herself. Consequently, investigators were misled, thus delaying the search for the actual culprit.

Other witnesses said they had seen a lone male in his 40s, wearing glasses, and clad in a raincoat despite the fact that it wasn't raining that day. This man was most likely Schwartz's killer.

The bifocals found near Schwartz's body turned out to be prison-issued so investigators began to look at recently-released convicts, particularly those with a record of sex crimes who bore some resemblance to the witness description of the assailant. The San Francisco office of the FBI assisted with the investigation but to no avail.

Interestingly, however, police in another jurisdiction did question a man who claimed to have been wounded in a convenience store attack; however, these officers did not have access to the Marin County all-points bulletin and, therefore, were unable to make a possible connection that this quiet man may have been responsible for Schwartz's murder. The next day the same wounded man visited an optometrist—Schwartz's doctor, in fact—to get a new pair of glasses. The previous day the police had questioned the doctor about Schwartz's prescription; however, he had no knowledge of the eyeglasses found at the scene of the crime. If he had then he might have recognized the "unique prescription" his new patient had.

During Schwartz's autopsy, the pathologist counted 12 separate stab wounds in her chest, likely made with a ten-inch knife. Several days later, some kids found a blood-crusted boning knife near the crime scene which was determined to have been purchased at a large chain grocery store. A television reporter had subsequently handled the knife, thus obliterating any fingerprints which might have been left by the murderer. Forensic evidence suggested that she, too, had been in a kneeling position when she died.

Anne Alderson

On 15 October 1980, 26-year-old former Peace Corps volunteer Anne Alderson entered the park to go for a jog and to demonstrate that the park was, for the most part, safe. Many witnesses saw her and the park's caretaker even remembered her sitting alone in the 5,000-seat amphitheater to watch the sunset. Earlier that day some of the same witnesses reported seeing a lone male around 50 years of age in the park "just standing around."

She was found the next day with a .38 caliber bullet in her head. This crime scene was different from the others in that Alderson was raped, then permitted to get dressed before being murdered. She was found propped, face up, against a rock with her right earring missing. Investigators believed that "her twisted arrangement" indicated that she may have been forced to kneel as well before being shot.

Mark McDermand—A Red Herring

Police thought they had the person responsible for her death when they investigated a double homicide on 16 October 1980, near Mount Tamalpais in Mill Valley. Mark McDermand, 35, and his brother, Edwin, 40, both lived with their mother, Helen, 75. At approximately 8:30 p.m. deputies responded to a call by a concerned friend. After forcing their way into the home, deputies found the body of a man lying in a hallway who was identified as Edwin. He had been shot in the head and chest. In a locked bedroom deputies found the deceased body of Helen, lying on the bed and covered by a blanket. She had a single bullet hole behind her left ear. Eight spent .22 caliber casings were found near the bodies.

Deputies found a small padlocked door that led to the basement. They discovered a note tacked to the inside of the door addressed to "Shitheels" that said that by the time the note and bodies were discovered it would be "way too late" and that the perpetrator would be found either "on the news or on a 'slab'". The note was signed "Mr. Hate."

Inside the room were spent .38 caliber casings, three .22 caliber bullets, and ankle holsters for a pistol and a knife. This smelly basement room had been Mark McDermand's bedroom and became the prime suspect.

The coroner said that the bodies had been dead for three or four days.

A few days later, the local newspaper and the Marin County Sheriff's Department received letters from an individual claiming responsibility for the double homicide and a handwriting expert stated that the same person who wrote the note at the McDermand's house also wrote these letters. In these letters, the writer stated that he would not be captured alive so on 24 October detectives devised a plan to lure him by running an ad directed at him with a phone number that said that if he surrendered he would be treated fairly.

McDermand called the number that evening and said that he was considering surrendering but that "he had some things to do first." He called again two days later with details about the murders; saying that he tried to kill his mother and brother quickly but miscalculated with Edwin, hence the multiple gunshot wounds. He said that he had to "stop Edwin from hurting others" and that he would turn himself in the next day.

When McDermand approached the police he was wearing a belt with a .38 caliber revolver and also had a set of thumb cuffs and three speed loaders. In his vehicle was a 12-gauge shotgun, a .22 caliber pistol, ammunition, a metal box containing several hypodermic syringes, and some insulin as McDermand was diabetic.

He told police that his brother was schizophrenic and had been deteriorating quickly so he borrowed the guns and then prepared to go on the run after the deed was done. McDermand said that he acted out of diminished capacity and that he, too, was schizophrenic and couldn't remember the murders or when he did he told several different stories.

Nevertheless, the jury found McDermand guilty of two counts of first-degree murder and he received the death penalty.

At the end of it all, investigators resolved his potential part in the trailside murders as none of his firearms matched the bullets found in the victims on Mount Tampalpais. That and the fact that the murders continued.

Shauna May

On 27 November 1980 25-year-old Shauna May disappeared from Point Reyes National Seashore Park while hiking. She was supposed to meet friends the following day to do more hiking. They had selected this area because it was several miles north of San Francisco and had not had the dubious distinction of having had a murder occur there recently. When she failed to show up, her friends alerted park officials.

Two days later her body was found by hikers who had seen her foot protruding from a shallow grave. She had been strangled with picture frame wire, shot three times in the head, and shoved into a shallow trench. She had also been raped.

Her body was found in close proximity to Diane O'Connell.

Diane O'Connell

The body of 22-year-old Diane O'Connell was found the same day and near May's body. She had disappeared a month earlier from the same area while hiking with friends as well and her body was rather decomposed. She had been raped, strangled with wire, and shot once in the head.

It was initially believed that the two women perhaps knew each other and were killed at around the same time as another hiker reported hearing four gunshots in that area of the park during the mid-afternoon.

The two women were laying together, face down. Their collective clothing was piled atop a backpack. A pair of underwear was stuffed into O'Connell's mouth. After investigating, it was determined that the two women did not know each other.

Richard Stowers and Cynthia Moreland

As if finding two bodies wasn't bad enough, police also discovered the bodies of 19-year-old Richard Towers and his girlfriend, 18-year-old Cynthia Moreland on the same day as May's and O'Connell's. The couple had been missing since 11 October, having last been seen by friends who they told that they were going to go hiking in the park. In fact, Stowers was in the Coast Guard and was reported as being AWOL.

Both victims had been murdered execution-style with bullets to the head.

An autopsy placed their time of death mere days before Alderson's, thus suggesting that there were two murderers or that a single killer had gone hunting for victims in two different areas. When ballistics determined that the bullet from Alderson's head matched those in both Stowers and Moreland, authorities knew there was just one single deadly predator.

Visitors were told not to go hiking alone; however, being together did not save Stowers and Moreland. Those who typically frequented the parks stayed away or went elsewhere until the murderer was caught.

Needless to say, the media frenzy that ensued wreaked panic throughout the area.

Was David Carpenter the Elusive Zodiac Killer?

Between December 1968 and July 1969 a man shot two couples on two separate occasions in Vallejo, California and then taunted detectives with phone calls claiming responsibility. One of the victims survived and was able to give police a description. Soon thereafter, editors of three San Francisco newspapers each received part of a strange letter also claiming to be from the killer. His message "consisted of a printed cryptogram composed of symbols and signed with a crossed-circle symbol" and all three of the letters had to be put together to decipher it. A local teacher was able to crack the code which stated that the killer enjoyed killing and it was his intention to continue doing so. He signed his letter "the Zodiac."

On 27 September 1969, while 20-year-old Bryan Hartnell and 22-year-old Cecelia Ann Shepard were picnicking at Lake Berryessa, a man in a black executioner's hood approached them. He stabbed Shepard ten times—five in the front and five in the back—and Hartnell six times in the back. He then called the police to report it.

Two weeks later the killer struck again, killing cab driver Paul Stine. The *San Francisco Chronicle* received a letter soon after accompanied by a torn piece of the shirt Stine was wearing at the time of his death. Investigators developed a number of suspects but none checked out. This serial killer was very clever and turned his escapades into multilayered games before he withdraw and maintained a low profile. This was quite disturbing for investigators who never knew when or where he would resurface.

In 1980, former FBI profiler John Douglas—who had been on the Zodiac case since it began—assisted sex crimes expert Special Agent Roy Hazelwood and San Francisco police to help create a profile of the Trailside Killer.

After examining the crime scene data and photos, Douglas concluded that the killer would be a local man who was shy, reclusive, and may have a speech impediment. Douglas also added that the murderer was likely socially awkward, white, intelligent, blue collar, and had spent time incarcerated. He was presumed to choose his victims out of opportunity rather than hunting the same type of victim. His modus operandi (MO) was to approach from behind and overwhelm his victim—"like a spider waiting for a bug to fly into his web." Douglas added that the killer would also have at least two of three specific background indicators common to many serial killers: bedwetting, fire-starting, and cruelty to animals. Finally, Douglas had said while the suspect likely committed rape in his past he had not killed anyone before his current murderous rampage. When questioned about the very specific speech impediment predictor, Douglas said that the secluded killing areas and method of approach indicated some type of shyness and/or shame and he believed it was due to some physical malady that really bothered the killer. Therefore, he attacked in the way he did to compensate for his handicap. While being very detailed, however, police still didn't have any potential suspects.

After Douglas returned to Quantico the Trailside Killer struck again.

Carpenter was ultimately cleared of any involvement with the Zodiac murders through fingerprint and handwriting analysis.

Ellen Hansen

On 29 March 1981, University of California at Davis undergraduate students Ellen Hansen and her boyfriend Stephen Haertle were ambushed in Henry Cowell State Park near Santa Cruz; another town that experienced a spate of murders during the early 1970s committed by Edmund Kemper, John Linley Frazier, and Herbert Mullin—all of whom were safely incarcerated at that time.

Carpenter approached the couple with a pistol in his hand and threatened the pair, insisting that Hansen permit him to rape her. Of course she refused, telling him off. Carpenter then opened fire, shooting Hansen point blank in the head twice and once in the shoulder. The assailant then shot Haertle and left him for dead. Haertle crawled for help despite wounds that ripped through his neck, a hand, and one eye. He proved instrumental in providing police with a partial description of the murderer: near 50, balding, approximately five-foot-ten to six-feet tall and approximately 170 pounds, with crooked yellow teeth, wearing dark glasses as well as a gold jacket with lettering on the back and a baseball cap. Haertle also remembered that the assailant had spoken in "quick, commanding sentences." This description differed considerably from the description of the Marin County killer; however, the MO was the same.

Other hikers reported that they had seen a man matching the description of the gunman in a red, late model, foreign car, running through the park after the gunshots had been fired.

Investigators were also able to lift some good shoeprint impressions to compare to a suspect when they got one.

Authorities released a composite drawing based upon Haertle's and other witness' descriptions in a number of newspapers to both alert people and hopefully get some leads. Four days later a woman called to describe a man she had met 26 years earlier on a cruise to Japan. She said that the purser on the cruise was a young man named David Carpenter who had been bothering her and her daughter with inappropriate behavior. She also recalled that he stuttered.

Presumably reading the paper and staying abreast with detectives' search for the Trailside Killer, Carpenter decided to grow a beard.

He then decided to kill much closer to home, enabling police to catch him.

Heather Scaggs

On 1 May 1981 police caught a break; however, it would come with another victim. On that day, 20-year-old Heather Scaggs disappeared on her way en route to buy a car with help from a coworker, one David Carpenter; they both worked at Econo Quick Print. She had told her boyfriend, Dan Pingle, that Carpenter "made a special point" of asking her to come alone when she came by to get the car and that his friend was selling it and Carpenter was going to help her purchase it. It was Pingle who informed police that she was missing. Luckily Scaggs had left Carpenter's address and phone number with him.

Scaggs' decomposing body was found on 24 May 1981 in Big Basin Redwood State Park, north of San Francisco. Ballistics from recovered bullets proved that she had been murdered with the same pistol used on Haertle and Hansen. She had also been raped and the DNA from the semen inside of her matched Carpenter.

Anna Menjivas

On 16 June 1981 a jaw bone later identified as belonging to Anna Menjivas was found by rock climbers in Castle Rock State Park. She had been missing since 28 December 1980 and was 17 years old at the time of her disappearance. She had worked part-time at the bank where Carpenter was a client and he often struck up conversation with her. Many believed that he only came into the bank to talk to her. Because the cause of death could not be established and there was scant evidence against him, he was not charged for her murder even though authorities were certain that he had killed her. Her name was added to the list of Carpenter's victims to bring his total to ten murders.

Investigation and Arrest

When police went to Carpenter's house to question him, they couldn't help but notice that Carpenter looked quite like the man in the composite sketch and that he had a shiny red Fiat.

Police discovered that Carpenter had not shown up on any released inmates' records where they initially searched due to a technicality: that he had been released by the state of California to serve a federal sentence and, while out on parole, was technically in federal custody. This issue resulted in the delay and subsequent difficulty in identifying him. That he was a habitual sex offender was another important factor not fully documented in his records.

The police department and FBI set up a surveillance van outside the house at 36 Sussex Street in San Francisco where Carpenter lived with his aging parents and also followed him on his errands, especially when he associated with other known criminals. They approached Carpenter who was walking down the street one day with a shopping bag in his hand to apprehend him. Initially confused, Carpenter then asked for a lawyer; at this point he was told that he was under arrest, to which he, strangely, begged, "Please don't hurt me."

Officers executed a search warrant on Carpenters home and car and found books about local hiking trails and over 60 maps. They talked to Carpenter's former fiancée who told them that he claimed that the gold jacket he once owned was stolen around the time of the Hansen murder; thus circumstantially placing him at the scene where Haertle and Hansen were shot. Further, Carpenter's car matched the one described by the surviving victim and several witnesses, he had the same optometrist as another victim, he had the right distinctive type of clothing, he had a record for violent sex offenses, he suffered from explosive rage and tried to change his appearance with different glasses and facial hair, and he matched many descriptions witnesses gave as the man who had been seen in the area of multiple attacks.

Haertle picked Carpenter's mugshot as the man who shot him and killed his girlfriend. Out of seven more witnesses present at a lineup, six picked him out although not all of them were sure. Police also conducted a car lineup with witnesses identifying Carpenter's Fiat.

He was formally charged with Hansen's murder and Haertle's attempted murder. At his arraignment Carpenter stuttered so badly that he had a difficult time answering the judges questions.

Police were never able to recover the .45 caliber gun that was used in several of his murders; however, a .38 caliber gun that Carpenter had sold to another man, who was on trial for robbery and gladly relinquished it to authorities, was later proven to be the firearm used in the last two murders.

Trial and Conviction

Carpenter's defense attorneys requested a change of venue due to the publicity surrounding his ten murders. However, if attorneys had thought it would make a difference they were mistaken. A change of venue would do nothing to eliminate the incriminating evidence police had against Carpenter. In April 1984, his Los Angeles trial began and on 6 July 1984, Carpenter was convicted of the Santa Cruz murders of Heather Scaggs and Ellen Hansen, and the attempted murder of

Stephen Haertle thanks to the damning evidence that his gun was the one responsible for their deaths. A second jury sentenced Carpenter to die in San Quentin's gas chamber based upon three special circumstances that warranted the death penalty: that he had committed multiple murders; that he had murdered during commission of rape; and that he had lain in wait for his victims. Judge Dion Morrow told the court that, "The defendant's entire life has been a continuous expression of violence and force almost beyond exception. I must conclude with the prosecution that if ever there was a case appropriate for the death penalty, this is it."

Carpenter's second trial began on 5 January 1988 in San Diego. On 10 May 1988, a San Diego jury found Carpenter guilty for five murders. Carpenter was also found guilty of two counts of rape and one count of attempted rape. This trial was different in that Carpenter himself took the stand in his own behalf. He was on the stand for seven days.

Marin County District Attorney Jerry Herman announced that he wouldn't file any charges against Carpenter for Kane's and Schwartz's murders due to inadequate evidence.

In 1994, potential juror misconduct in the second trial was brought to light in that the jury forewoman had known about Carpenter's convictions in Los Angeles for the Santa Cruz murders and had concealed this fact during voir dire for the Marin County trial. Carpenter was not retried as he had already been sentenced to death for other murders. On 6 March 1995 the California Supreme Court refused to give Carpenter a new trial. Justice Armand Arabian said that it was virtually impossible to keep secrets in cases such as this and that he believed that the juror's knowledge had not unduly biased the jury.

In 1997, the California Supreme Court upheld Carpenter's death sentence for the Scaggs and Hansen murders and on 29 November 199 they upheld Carpenter's death penalty from his second trial, with six of the seven justices agreeing that he had a fair trial for the five Marin County murders and had, in fact, been sentenced properly.

In December 2009, San Francisco police reexamined evidence from the 21 October 1979 murder of Mary Frances Bennett. Bennett was 23 years old at the time she was killed. She had been jogging near the Palace of the Legion of Honor in Land's End Park in San Francisco when she was ambushed and stabbed to death. Police reported that she had been stabbed at least 25 times in her chest, neck, and back. Her "butchered" corpse was found under a thin layer of dirt and leaves. In February 2010 San Francisco police confirmed that DNA collected from that murder was sent to the Department of Justice and was subsequently matched to Carpenter.

He remains a suspect in the murders of Edna Kane and Barbara Schwartz.

Aftermath

Some have speculated that Carpenter wasn't technically a serial killer but a serial rapist who killed his victims to eliminate witnesses so as not to return to prison.

Carpenter's case provided the background for Joyce Maynard's 2013 novel, *After Her*.

A series of geocaching caches have been placed throughout Mount Tamalpais in commemoration of Carpenter's victims.

TOY BOX KILLER

David Parker Ray was a suspected American serial killer and known torturer and serial rapist of women; suspected because no bodies were ever found. However, he was accused by his accomplices of murdering a number of women and law enforcement officials estimate that he is responsible for as many as 60 deaths in and near Truth or Consequences, New Mexico. Ray purchased and refitted a trailer into what he called his "toy box" which was replete with a number of sex toys and torture items for his victims. He also played a very disturbing audiotape for all of his victims explaining what they will be enduring at his hand. Ray was finally arrested after one of his victims managed to escape after three days of torture. Ray stood trial for kidnapping and sexual torture and was sentenced to 224 years in prison; however, he suffered a fatal heart attack while incarcerated at Lea County Correctional Facility in Hobbs, New Mexico, on 28 May 2002.

Early Life

David Parker Ray was born on 6 November 1939, in Belen, New Mexico. He was named David after his uncle David who was accidentally shot in the heart at the age of 13 by his 15-year-old brother Alden just one year earlier. Ray's grandmother believed him to be a reincarnation of her dead son.

Ray's father, Cecil, was an alcoholic and was very abusive to both Ray and his sister Peggy—who was one year his junior—as well as their mother, Nettie. When Ray was ten years old his father left his mother and moved to Albuquerque. They were divorced soon thereafter. When Nettie decided to stay with her own parents, Ray and Peggy were shipped off to their paternal grandparents, Ethan and Dolly Ray. In the six years Ray and Peggy lived with their grandparents they saw their father twice and their mother only a handful of times. Consequently, there were no maternal bonds between Nettie and her children. In fact, Ray said that he didn't get much affection or attention at all during his childhood.

Ethan was a strict disciplinarian who insisted on the utmost standards of dress and behavior and, as such, the children were required to do ranch chores both before and after school and even though the Rays were not very well off, Ethan made sure his grandchildren were clean and presentable. He was also a devout fundamentalist Christian and made sure to instill within his grandchildren his religious beliefs. Any nonadherence to his rules resulted in physical punishment.

Ray attended Mountainair High School in Mountainair, New Mexico, where he was often bullied for his awkwardness and shyness, especially around girls. Ray commented that he didn't have his first date until he was 18 years old. He was also tormented for being soft-spoken and for having to keep his shirt buttoned all the way to the top—per his grandfather's instructions—when all of the other boys had a few top buttons undone. Ray was also a poor student.

Neighbor Audie Miranda always tried to look out for Ray. He would tell the bullies to leave him alone and stated that even though Ray could defend himself, he remained docile, not liking or believing in violence which was ironic considering what Ray would become. The two became close friends and spent a lot of time together on the Ray ranch riding horses, playing cowboys and Indians, and playing desert hide-and-seek.

Ray always had a love of the outdoors.

Miranda would later say that he believed that Ray's ultra-strict upbringing took a toll on his friend. Miranda even commented that he, himself, was scared of Ethan.

Dolly was not much better. Ray said that he hated her and that she "didn't have a clue."

At the age of 12, Ray began building and setting off bombs and other explosives he fashioned in the woods behind his grandparents' house. He said he blew up a lot of tree stumps as a child.

When Ray was 13 his grandparents gave him a Cushman Pacemaker motor scooter. He discovered within himself a natural aptitude for mechanics and delighted in taking it apart and then reassembling it. The once shy and timid Ray became more confident, especially when his classmates who used to torment him needed his services to fix their scooters.

Some accounts state that Ray began to use and abuse alcohol and drugs while in high school. It was also around this time he began to fantasize about raping, torturing, and murdering women. He said that the few times his father would come visit them, he would bring true detective magazines which Ray enjoyed reading. He began having his fantasies which always involved broken bottles. His sister stumbled upon Ray's sadomasochistic drawings as well as erotic photographs of acts of bondage.

At the age of 15 Ray fashioned his own little dungeon under a large piñon pine tree with a hangman's noose and a collection of broken beer bottles he "planned to use on girls someday." He also admitted to digging a hole and engaging in intercourse with the ground when he was lonesome.

After high school, Ray worked as an auto mechanic.

He married in 1959, joking that he was practically a virgin at that time, and joined the United States Army a year later where he was sent to Korea. The Rays had a son in 1960 and Ray had to return home on emergency leave because his wife was leaving the baby alone when she went out to party. He filed for divorce and sought sole custody. His mother, Opel, and stepfather, Cecil, raised Ray's son until Ray was honorably discharged from the military.

Ray married a second time in 1962 when he was 22 years old and a mere 90 days later he went back to court and filed for divorce again because they just didn't "click".

In 1966, Ray married a third time; to a woman named Glenda Burdine. They were married 15 years and had a daughter named Glenda Jean—who would go by "Jesse"—in 1969. Jesse remembered her father as being gone quite a bit, having worked for the railroad, and of having an unusual fetish for padded leather straps and other bondage fare. She said that kids were naturally curious and while they knew about it, it was not a topic to be discussed.

In sum, Ray married four times, was divorced four times, and had two children.

Ray met Cindy Lea Hendy in 1997 when he was 57; she was 20 years his junior. Originally from Washington, Hendy and her boyfriend John Youngblood moved to Truth or Consequences, New Mexico, on the run from the law for grand theft, forgery, and drug offenses, leaving her three children behind. As she had already served time in jail, she was not keen on returning.

The Crimes

The "Toy Box"

Ray spent over $100,000 on his homemade torture chamber he called his "toy box" that he constructed inside of an old white 15-feet-by-25-feet cargo trailer on his Elephant Butte, New Mexico, property. Elephant Butte is a resort town of approximately 2,000 residents, located along an 18-mile-long, 36,000-acre reservoir.

The trailer was stocked with what he referred to as his "friends": bully whips, pulleys, leather straps, metal clamps, bars which spread the victim's legs, surgical knifes and saws which he used to torture women. Inside this trailer were also numerous sex toys, syringes, detailed diagrams that showed different methods for inflicting pain and torture, and a homemade electrical generator. Ray also mounted a mirror on the ceiling above the gynecologist table upon which he strapped his victims because he wanted them to see everything that was done to them.

He also played a recorded audiotape of himself for his victims whenever they regained consciousness. It began with:

*"Hello there, b*tch. Are you comfortable right now? I doubt it. Wrists and ankles chained. Gagged. Probably blind folded. You are disoriented*

*and scared, too, I would imagine. Perfectly normal, under the circumstances. For a little while, at least, you need to get your sh*t together and listen to this tape. It is very relevant to your situation. I'm going to tell you, in detail, why you have been kidnapped, what's going to happen to you and how long you'll be here. I don't know the details of your capture, because this tape is being created July 23rd, 1993, as a general advisory tape for future female captives. The information I'm going to give you is based on my experience dealing with captives over a period of several years. If, at a future date, there are any major changes in our procedures, the tape will be upgraded. Now, you are obviously here against your will, totally helpless, don't know where you're at, don't know what's gonna happen to you. You're very scared or very pissed off. I'm sure that you've already tried to get your wrists and ankles loose, and know you can't. Now you're just waiting to see what's gonna happen next."*

The rest of the tape involves Ray setting forth his "rules" and "procedures" by telling his victims everything—in graphic detail—that would be done to them to include being raped and sodomized by Ray and his friends, engaging in bestiality, being shocked with electricity, and being poked and prodded with a multitude of surgical instruments and sex toys; essentially, being their sex slave to do with whatever they want. The actual recording is widely available online, quite long, and not for the faint of heart as it is extremely explicit.

In the audiotape Ray describes himself as a "dungeon master" who was affiliated with the Church of Satan and that his slaves were for members of his "congregation."

There was also a videotape showing Ray and his girlfriend Cindy Lea Hendy performing such acts of torture upon a female victim who screamed the entire time.

Psychological torture was also important to Ray. He would blindfold his victims, subject them to brainwashing, use fear tactics, and occasional small favors to keep them "off balance".

Many experts classify Ray as a sexual sadist who finds excitement and pleasure from inflicting pain upon a nonconsensual, submissive and inducing them into altered states of consciousness such as when they pass out from the pain. Such a predilection often forms during adolescence; however, experts do not know exactly what causes one to become a sexual sadist.

Ray had multiple accomplices during this time; including, allegedly, several of his girlfriends, particularly his latest girlfriend, Hendy.

During the investigation Hendy allegedly had told a friend—while she was under the influence of alcohol—that she had willingly participated in Ray's attacks because of the adrenaline rush she got from them. She allegedly confided to this person that "there were four to six people who had been killed, dismembered, and tossed into Elephant Butte Lake." While the friend did not initially believe her, after Ray and Hendy were arrested and the details of the crimes were released, he gave statements to police and the media.

Marie Parker

On 5 July 1997, 22-year-old Marie Parker and her two daughters—ages four and five—were evicted from their apartment for non-payment of rent. They were living in a pup tent on the western shore of Elephant Butte Lake at a campsite called Hot Springs Cove; just north of Ray's trailer. In fact, she had borrowed the tent from him and when her campsite became too messy for the fastidious Ray, he had something to say about it.

Parker was a methamphetamine and cocaine junkie and her main supplier was Ray's daughter Jesse. Ray abducted Parker and took her to his toy box where he raped and tortured her for three days after which he gave Yancy a rope and told him that they "were finished" with her. He then told Yancy to kill her which Yancy admitted to doing. They buried the body in a remote area and Ray threatened Yancy's life if he ever told anyone.

Later, when police took Yancy to the area where Parker's body was allegedly dumped, they could not find any evidence. Yancy stated that Ray probably moved the body.

Police found Parker's abandoned car in the parking lot of the Blue Waters Saloon.

Cynthia Vigil

Cynthia Vigil had been working as a prostitute along Central Avenue (Highway 66) at around 10:00 a.m. when her pimp introduced her to Ray and Hendy in a red recreational vehicle. Ray offered Vigil $20 for oral sex and when she entered the vehicle, Ray produced a police badge and told Vigil that she was under arrest for solicitation. Ray and Hendy handcuffed, gagged, and chained Vigil to a fixture inside of the camper. After a few minutes he pulled the vehicle over and then proceeded to cut off all of her clothing, put a metal dog collar around her neck, place her in shackles, and then slipped a leather mask over her head with no eye openings and a zipper for the mouth. She was also told if she resisted she would be shocked.

When they reached Ray's house, after driving for an hour, Vigil said that she was chained to a bed and was made to listen to Ray's infamous five-minute audiotape before being forced to have sex with both Ray and Hendy. Next, Vigil said that Ray put gravy "up" her and had his German shepherd lick it off. Vigil then had her knees attached to a bar, forcing her legs open and was then "measured" with dildoes that had markings on them before having her breasts and genitals shocked with a portable generator. The entire time Hendy had a gun pointed at her.

The next morning, Vigil was taken at gunpoint to the bathroom to relieve herself and then taken back to the bed, fresh and clean white sheets atop it, where her mouth and eyes were duct taped and she was hog-tied with an elaborate collection of interconnected leather straps. A rope was then attached to a pulley from the ceiling and Vigil's entire body was lifted three feet into the air.

The duct tape was ripped from her eyes and she saw her horrified face staring back at her from a video monitor. She said that Ray tied her legs open and proceeded to whip her with a leather belt, whips, and a cat-o' nine tails. Vigil said that the beating excited Ray who then violated her with a "horrendous looking dildo" and took pictures of her suspended body with the toys inside of her.

Later that day he attached an elaborate system of clamps and pulleys to her breasts and genitalia and proceeded to shock her. Her convulsions caused the pulleys to exert force on the clamps. After taking the excruciating pain for as long as she could, she lost consciousness.

For the next two days Vigil was subjected to sexual torture until she was able to escape.

On 22 March 1999, Cynthia Vigil escaped after being abducted by Ray and enduring a three-day torture ordeal. She was able to escape one morning after Ray had left for work and Hendy had left the keys on a nearby table when the latter went into another room to talk on the phone. Vigil—chained to the wall in the den—managed to use her legs and feet to pull the table toward her and get the keys; however, Hendy noticed her efforts and a fight ensued. Vigil was able to free herself while Hendy beat her and even after being hit in the head with a lamp, Vigil managed to stab Hendy in the back of the neck with an icepick she found on the floor. When Hendy fell to the ground, Vigil escaped the house naked save for an iron slave collar and padlocked chains, and began to run down Bass Road in Elephant Butte. Since she had just been taken three days ago, Vigil had not been taken out to the toy box yet.

Vigil was spotted by a couple of passing motorists who did not know what to make of the woman and didn't stop. Vigil finally surprised a woman at home in her trailer watching television who called the police for her. Vigil was then taken to the Sierra Vista

County Hospital emergency room where the chains were cut off and her battered body was cared for.

When police went to Ray's home, they found bloodied sheets in one bedroom with a broken lamp and broken window, thus corroborating Vigil's claims. A pulley device with hooks and chains was mounted on the ceiling and there was a long, coffin-like box along the side of the bed. Large sex toys were on the dresser.

Arrest and Investigation

After Vigil's escape, Ray and Hendy were arrested off Springfield Road in his red Toyota camper. They claimed that they had kidnapped Vigil in an effort to break her of her heroin addiction. Ray and Hendy were taken to nearby Truth or Consequences—formerly Hot Springs—New Mexico and housed in the Cooper Police Training Center.

Both Ray and Hendy were charged with 12 counts consisting of aggravated kidnapping, conspiracy, and aggravated battery and held on $1 million bail.

Soon after Ray was arrested, New Mexico State Police took the case over from the Truth or Consequences Police Department and Agent Wesley LaCuesta—a five-year veteran of the Criminal Assault and Violent Crimes Division—was called on to assist in the investigation. He left his Las Cruces office and headed north to Truth or Consequences.

LaCuesta interviewed Vigil at the hospital. He observed many small cuts on her extremities, injuries to her breasts, welts on her back, and evidence of her being handcuffed.

By early April 1999, over 100 New Mexico State Police and FBI agents were all over Ray's property looking for human remains.

Eleven days after his arrest, Patty Rust committed suicide after assisting law enforcement personnel with detailed drawings of the toy box over the course of four days. Prosecutor Jim Yontz wondered why the FBI would send a woman into a torture chamber where many women had likely been frightened to death by Ray and the torture he inflicted upon them. He then went to visit the toy box. Inside he found a ghastly collection of sex toys, medical devices, whips, clamps, chains, pulleys, rods, saws, and other items for bondage and sadomasochism; in addition to detailed drawings of how Ray liked to torture his victims, medical books on the female anatomy, and, perhaps most damning, a videotape dating back to 1993 showing a woman being tortured.

There was also a television monitor in the right corner of the toy box so Ray's victims could see what he was doing to them if they looked at the monitor while they were secured to the table. He also had a video camera focused upon the table recording everything he was doing. Photographs of the torture he had inflicted upon prior victims decorated the walls, as well as a bunch of dolls which were "strung up in various states of bondage and torture." In addition to the medical texts, Ray had a copy of Brett Easton Ellis' *American Psycho*; a novel detailing violent assaults inflicted by a man when he needed to release steam from his high-stress life that was also made into a film starring Christian Bale. The novel contains very disturbing descriptions of torture. It was presumed that Ray compared himself to the "protagonist" in the novel as he saw himself as in control and his victims as "expendable pawns in his game", even going so far as to call his victims "packages."

With respect to the videotape depicting the torture of one of Ray's victims, the police were able to find the woman on the tape: Kelly Garrett, who had been married mere days before being abducted by Ray and Hendy. Garrett had been held hostage, raped, and tortured for three days before being drugged and left on the side of the road not far from her in-laws' house. Believing Garrett had been out on a drug binge, she was asked to leave and subsequently moved back to Colorado. Investigators found her in Colorado and she stated that she had amnesia for a long time, only recently—as in the past year—remembering what Ray and Hendy had done to her.

The publicity surrounding the case prompted another victim to come forward with her story. Angelica Montano recounted her ordeal at Ray's hands just one month ago.

Angelica Montano

Montano said that she was a casual acquaintance of both Ray and Hendy and had gone to their house on 17 February 1999, looking to borrow cake mix. She said that Ray left the room and then returned with a knife and told her that she was being kidnapped. When Montano looked over at Hendy, she saw the woman holding a gun, pointed at her. She knew they were serious.

Montano said that the couple grabbed, bound, and stripped her before strapping her to a bed and placing a metal collar on her. She said they then attached electrodes to her breasts and shocked her multiple times in addition to "abus[ing] her with various sexual implements." She then said that Ray forced her to give him oral sex.

After having been chained naked to the bed for three days and being subjected to sexual abuse, it was time for Montano to visit the toy box. Ray removed her handcuffs and led her to the bathroom with a long metal leash attached to the dog collar. He bathed her "like a dog, with a chain and everything" Montano would later say. When she was clean, Hendy applied makeup to her face and then draped a robe over her captive's shoulders before Ray and Hendy led her out into the trailer.

In the smaller trailer—the toy box—Montano was strapped to a gynecologist table where she was subjected to additional electric shocks to her genitalia as well as other instances of sexual assault. She said that she repeatedly begged Ray and Hendy to release her and on the fourth day they relented. She was drugged and taken miles away from Ray's property and dumped on a local highway in the desert where a police officer found her.

Even though Montano did, in fact, report the incident to the police, there had been no follow up. When she saw that Ray and Hendy had been arrested, Montano contacted the police again.

Accomplices

In addition to Hendy, investigators discovered two other accomplices: Ray's daughter Glenda Jean "Jesse" Ray; and Dennis Roy Yancy. Yancy and Hendy had dated in the past.

Yancy admitted to strangling Marie Parker—a former girlfriend—after Ray kidnapped and tortured her. Ray videotaped the murder. Yancy also confessed to seeing photographs of one of Ray's ex-wives in various bondage positions as well as watching Ray torture a woman inside the toy box but that he thought it was consensual. Yancy was subsequently convicted of second-degree murder and conspiracy to commit first-degree murder. He received two 15-year sentences. Jesse was also tried and convicted of kidnapping for sexual torture. She was sentenced to seven years and served three, the rest of the time she was on parole.

Hendy was charged with 25 felonies and was looking at 197 years in prison. To save herself, she agreed to plead no contest and testify against Ray and Yancy in exchange for five felony counts and a 36-year sentence. In the Seventh District Court of New Mexico Hendy pled guilty to two counts of first-degree kidnapping for Vigil and Montano, two counts of sexual penetration (rape) in the second degree for the two women, and one count of conspiracy to commit second-degree kidnapping.

Over 100 FBI agents were sent to search Ray's property but they were unable to identify any human remains. Several bones were located but they proved to be of animal origin. Collecting evidence from Ray's home and toy box proved daunting due to the sheer number of items he had amassed for his tortuous pleasure. In one interview, New Mexico Public Safety Director Darren White told reporters that the evidence inside the toy box was "very disturbing stuff" and "literally made my stomach turn."

It was later discovered that Ray would drug his victims with sodium pentothal and phenobarbital to induce amnesia to prevent them from being able to report what had happened to them when they were released. In Kelly Garrett's case, she was unsure about her own recollections of the torture and accompanying nightmares; that is, until the FBI contacted her and, soon thereafter, she was able to remember—in vivid detail—what Ray did to her so she could testify against him in court.

In his recording, Ray described his whole philosophy about drugging his victims and why getting an accurate body count of those victims he killed is impossible. Ray said:

*"If I killed every b*tch that we kidnapped, there'd be bodies strung all over the country. And besides, I don't like killin' a girl, unless it is absolutely necessary. So I've devised a safe, alternate method of disposal. I had plenty of b*tches to practice on over the years, so I've pretty well got it down pat. And I enjoy doin' it. I get off on mind games. After we get completely through with you, you're gonna be drugged up real heavy, with a combination of Sodium Pentothal and Phenobarbital. They are both hypnotic drugs that will make you extremely susceptible to hypnosis, autohypnosis and hypnotic suggestion. You're gonna be kept drugged a couple of days, while I play with your mind. By the time I get through brainwashing you, you're not gonna remember a fu*kin' thing about this little adventure. You won't remember this place, us, or what has happened to you. There won't be any DNA evidence, because you'll be bathed, and both holes between your legs will be thoroughly flushed out. You'll be dressed, sedated, and turned loose on some country road, bruised, heh, sore all over, but nothing that won't heal up in a week or two. The thought of being brainwashed may not be appealing to you, but we been doin' it a long time and it works. And it's the lesser of two evils. I'm sure that you would prefer that, in lieu of being strangled or having your throat cut."*

One can only imagine the pure horror coursing through his victims' minds as they lay, chained atop his torture table, hearing—in very graphic detail—about what they will be enduring.

Trials and Convictions

The press jumped all over the case and soon discovered that everyone who seemingly knew Ray said that he seemed like a "regular" guy. He did not have any criminal record, nor were there any reports about potentially suspicious activities on his property which he leased from the park service. However, reports from the police indicated that he was considerably worse and darker than he initially seemed.

State District Judge Neil Mertz decided that Ray would undergo three separate trials: for Cynthia Vigil, for Angelica Montano, and for Kelly Garrett. The Vigil trial was set to start on 28 March 2000, in Tierra Amarilla. Judge Mertz suppressed Ray's early interviews with the New Mexico State Police and FBI and also banned the media from the voir dire. Just after jury selection, Ray allegedly suffered a heart attack and was taken to a hospital in Las Cruces. The judge postponed the trial for another week and then there were additional delays and several FBI expert witnesses were excluded.

Then, unexpectedly, Judge Mertz decided to start Garrett's trial for her 1996 kidnapping and torture even though it was the weakest case, evidence-wise. Nevertheless, Judge Mertz scheduled it for the end of May. Of course, Ray was pleased with the delays, not to mention Judge Mertz's exclusion of Ray's printed sheet of procedures for handling his slaves as well as all devices found in the trailer for Garrett's trial since nobody could prove they were there in 1996. This left the prosecution with the videotape and the victim's testimony.

When Vigil's trial was actually conducted, it ended in a mistrial because some jurors were not convinced that the women were completely held against their will and there was a subsequent retrial that resulted in convictions for all 12 counts with which Ray was charged.

Montano's trial was delayed indefinitely because, unfortunately, she was rushed to an Albuquerque hospital on 7 May 2001 with pneumonia where she died an hour later from heart failure. She was only 28 years old. As she was one of only three living, known witnesses who were going to testify against Ray, Montano's death dealt a huge blow to the prosecution. However, prosecutor Jim Yontz was prepared to try Ray for Montano's kidnapping and torture by utilizing videotaped statements she had made at a preliminary hearing on 15 and 16 April 1999.

When prosecutors started "closing in" on his daughter Jesse who assisted with some of Ray's earlier kidnappings, Ray decided to take a plea bargain. He received a sentence of 224 years in prison.

Ray suffered a fatal heart attack while incarcerated at Lea County Correctional Facility in Hobbs, New Mexico, on 28 May 2002.

Aftermath

Yancy was paroled in 2010 after serving 11 years of his sentence; however, his release was delayed because of difficulties stemming from his parole plan which had to be established before release. Three months after he was released in 2011, he was charged with violating his parole and subsequently returned to prison and required to serve his entire sentence until 2021.

Ray is suspected of murdering his one-time business partner, Billy Bowers. The two men bought, restored, and sold cars. On 22 September 1988, Bowers disappeared and his family immediately offered a $5,000 reward for any information leading to his safe return. On 28 September 1989, a fisherman found a male body floating in McCrea Canyon which is along the eastern shore of Elephant Butte Lake. The body was wrapped in a blue tarp and secured to two heavy boat anchors. It had a single bullet hole to the head and $49.47 in a pocket but no identification. There were no missing persons reports for a five-foot-ten-inch male in his late-30's or early-40's so the John Doe remained unidentified for over a decade until Cindy Hendy told police that Ray had murdered Bowers. Hendy admitted that Ray confessed the murder to her and told her that since then he had learned to open the victims' stomachs so they would "stay down" when submerged in water and not float to the surface as was the case with Bowers.

When the body was exhumed and dental records compared, the John Doe was, in fact, Bowers. His son Michael was able to retrieve the body of his long-lost father for a proper burial and some closure.

In November 2002, state police officially opened the toy box to the public in the hopes that renewed media attention might help identify additional victims. Inside were signs that said "Satan's Den" and "Bondage Room." The obstetrical table was still there with all of its clamps, leg stretchers, electric wires, chains, and straps. A steel cabinet held numerous surgical instruments and the coffin-shaped box used to terrorize and contain victims was nearby. Ray's meticulous records detailing what he did to his victims was also available. To ensure that none of his victims escaped, Ray had devised an elaborate alarm system and had written instructions to ensure that all straps were secure prior to leaving the toy box.

However, with Ray dead, the investigation went cold, especially since no bodies were ever found, no possible victims were identified, and no suspicious deaths which might have been loosely linked to Ray were solved. Despite the lack of any dead bodies, he is oft-labeled in numerous sources of literature as a serial killer.

According to Jim Fielder in his 2003 book *Slow Death*, both Vigil and Garrett went on to form relationships and start families of their own.

As recently as 2012, additional evidence has been uncovered which indicated there may be additional victims.

www.ingramcontent.com/pod-product-compliance
Lightning Source LLC
Chambersburg PA
CBHW021446150726
47989CB00001B/423